SCOTT MORSE

Visitations™

Preface

So here's the thing:

I've always been a sucker for the unexplained, everything from Nessie living under Urquhart Castle to Tesla frying half of Siberia to Mokele-mbembe causing food poisoning in the Likouala swamp region.... and yes, even ghost stories. Specters, spooks, poltergeists, apparitions. Gotta love 'em. I'll drop dead if I ever see one, mind you, but it's really not a concern. See, I'm convinced they'll never show for me.

I want it too much.

They (specters, spooks, poltergeists, apparitions) no doubt sit around looking for people to freak out, occasionally happen upon me, and decide I wouldn't be any fun, simply because I *want* them to be there. Why convert the believers, eh?

So here's what I did:

With my love of ghosts and such in mind, I wanted to play with a story, *this* story, by pulling in inspiration from a few other sources, and keep a feeling of human emotion to it....really bring forth some *characters*. Structurally, I felt I should pan out a bit. I looked to how Akira Kurosawa could play concepts off of emotions with films like *RASHOMON* and *DREAMS*, retaining down to earth character moments and using them to push the situations at hand into something very symbolic....and very touching. I drew upon Masaki Kobayashi's *KWAIDAN* as a guide for integrating the human condition with the possibility of afterlife contact, to make the apparitions in my story not the bogeymen of horror films, but the sort of spirits that are whispered of around the campfire, or in dimly lit rooms much too late at night, when the air around you is very thick with the feeling of someone watching you, someone that realizes you want to see them maybe a little too much....

....but you won't see them.

Why convert the believers?

Scott Morse
Burbank, 1998

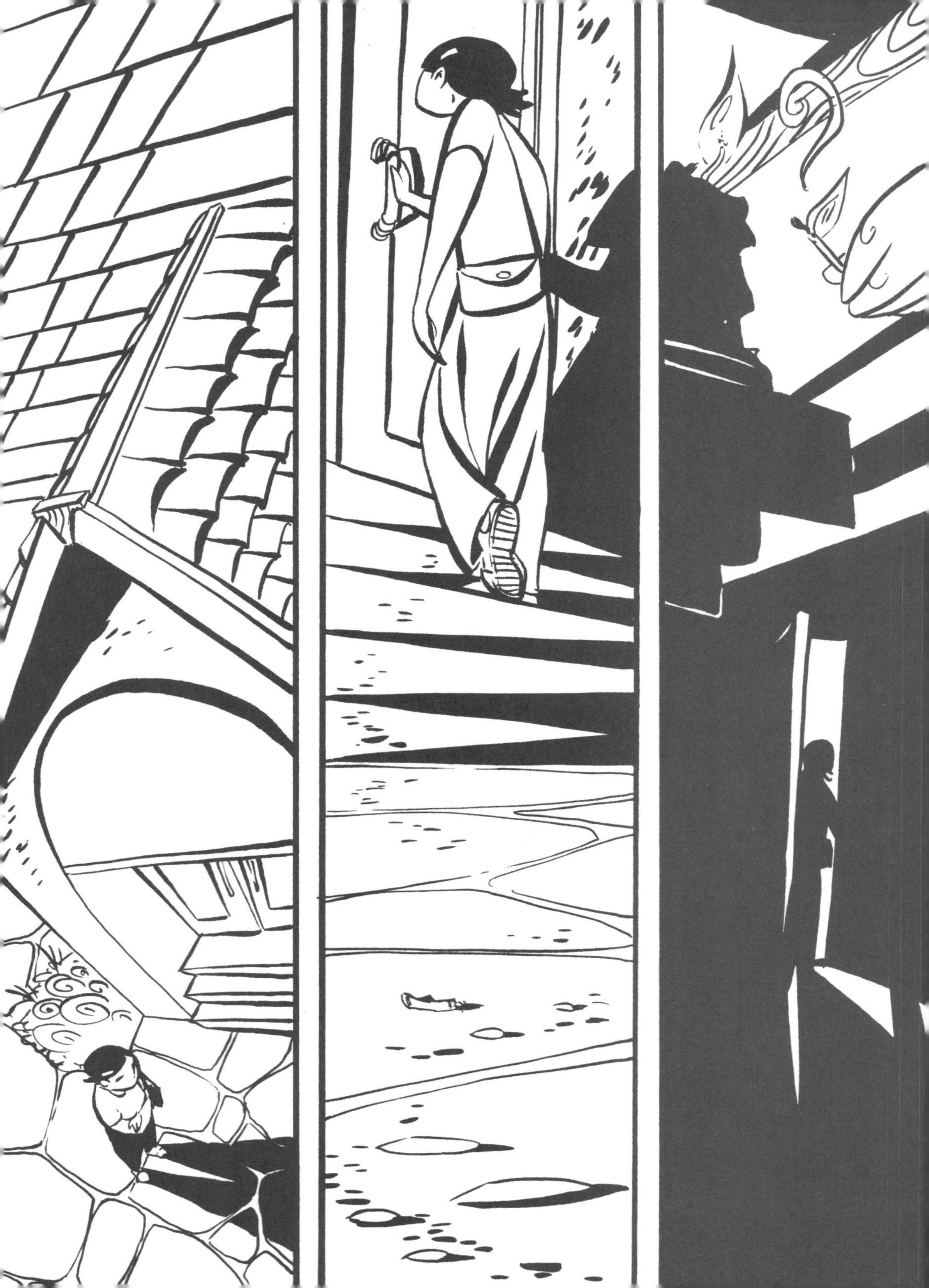

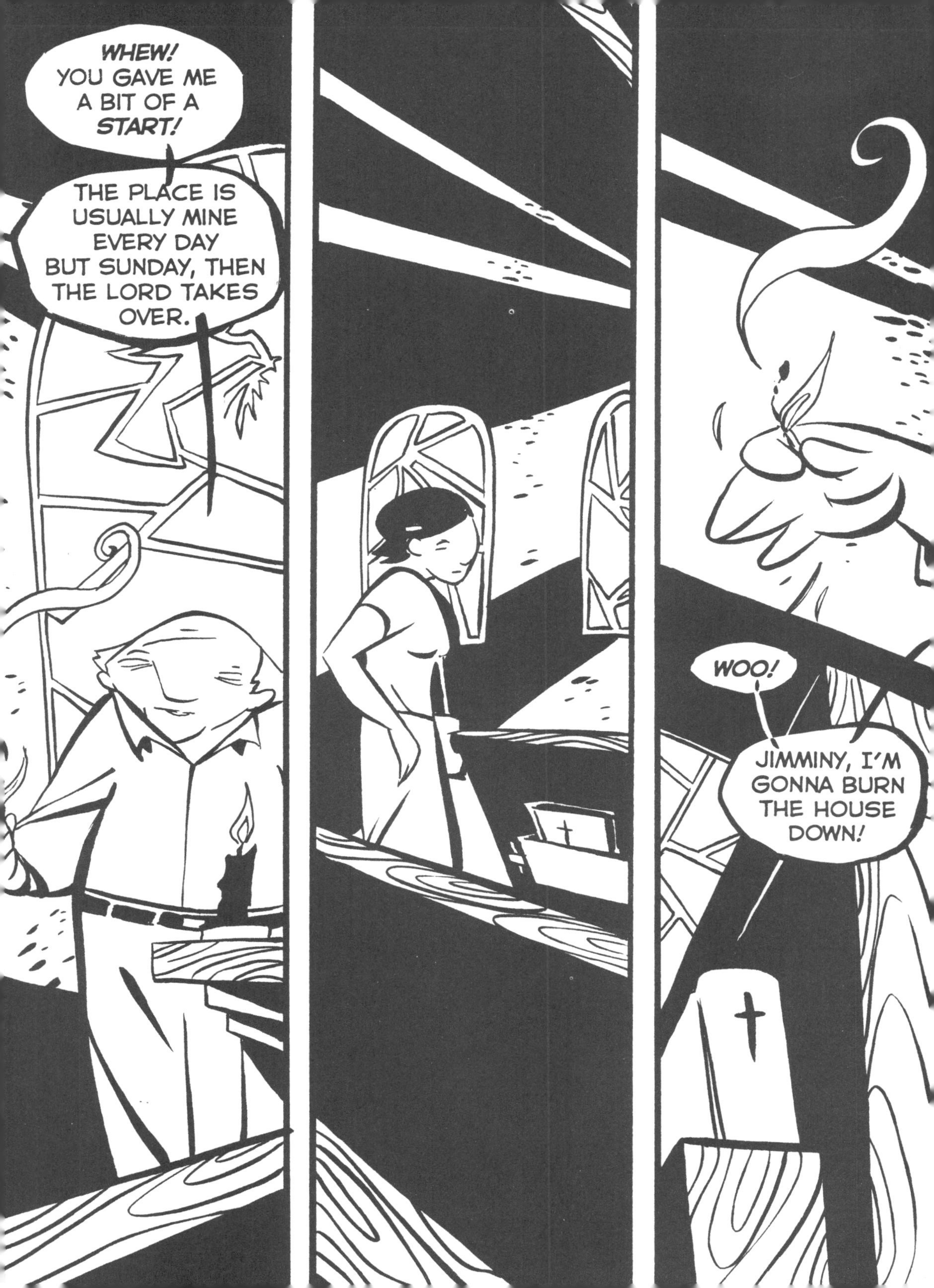
WHEW! YOU GAVE ME A BIT OF A START!
THE PLACE IS USUALLY MINE EVERY DAY BUT SUNDAY, THEN THE LORD TAKES OVER.
WOO!
JIMMINY, I'M GONNA BURN THE HOUSE DOWN!

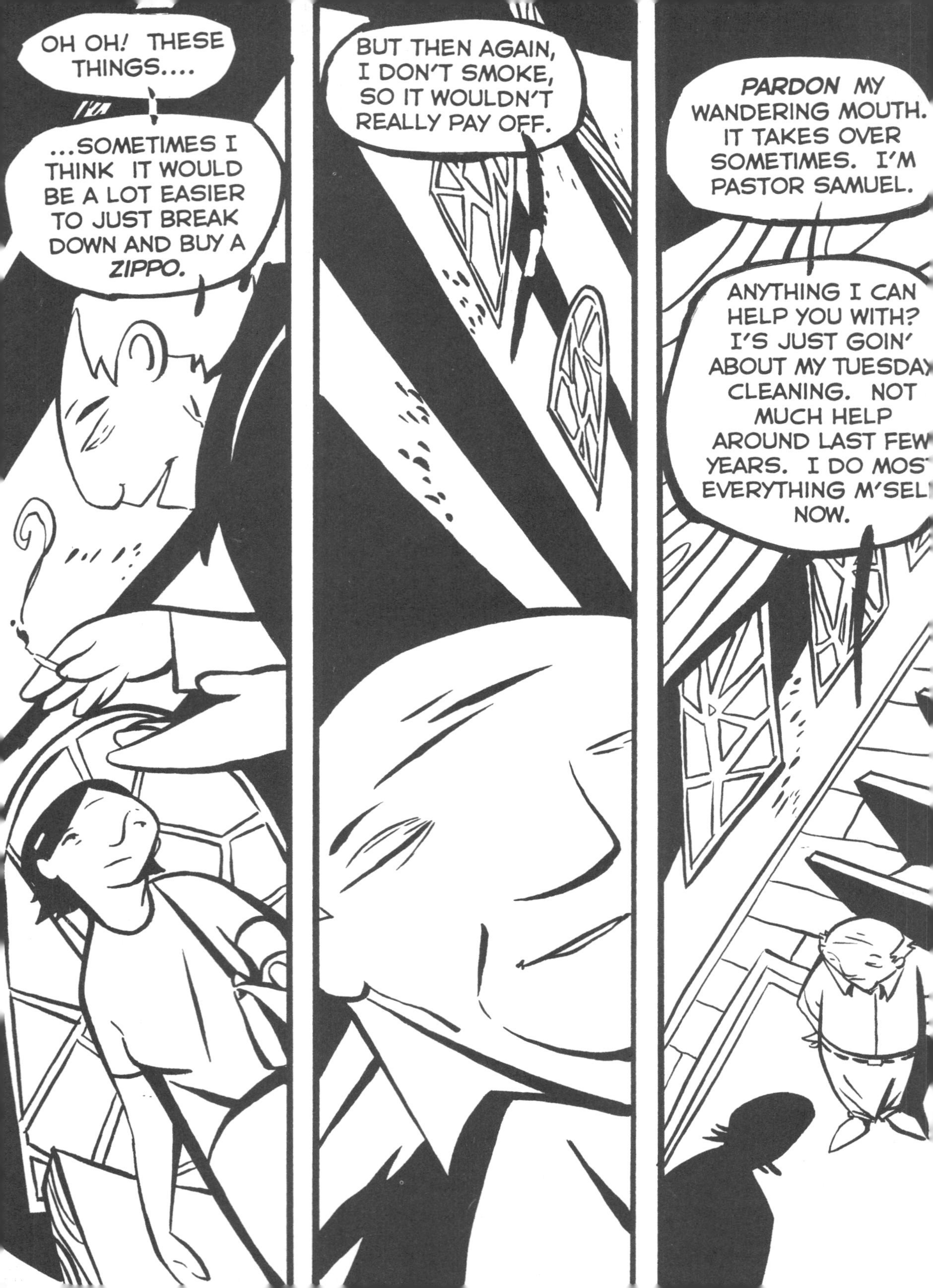

OH OH! THESE THINGS....
...SOMETIMES I THINK IT WOULD BE A LOT EASIER TO JUST BREAK DOWN AND BUY A *ZIPPO.*
BUT THEN AGAIN, I DON'T SMOKE, SO IT WOULDN'T REALLY PAY OFF.
PARDON MY WANDERING MOUTH. IT TAKES OVER SOMETIMES. I'M PASTOR SAMUEL.
ANYTHING I CAN HELP YOU WITH? I'S JUST GOIN' ABOUT MY TUESDAY CLEANING. NOT MUCH HELP AROUND LAST FEW YEARS. I DO MOST EVERYTHING M'SELF NOW.

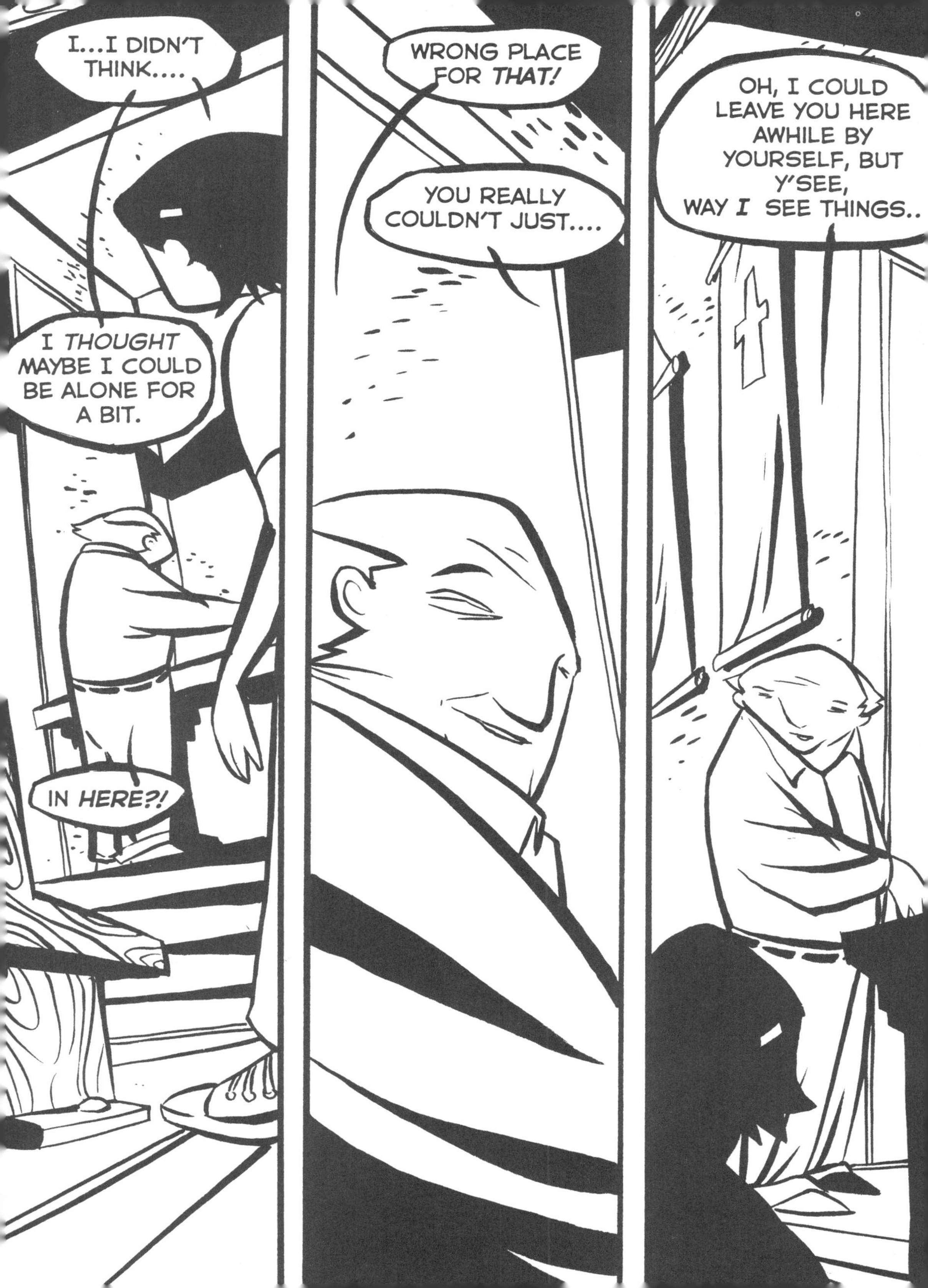
I...I DIDN'T THINK....
I THOUGHT MAYBE I COULD BE ALONE FOR A BIT.
IN HERE?!
WRONG PLACE FOR THAT!
YOU REALLY COULDN'T JUST....
OH, I COULD LEAVE YOU HERE AWHILE BY YOURSELF, BUT Y'SEE, WAY I SEE THINGS..

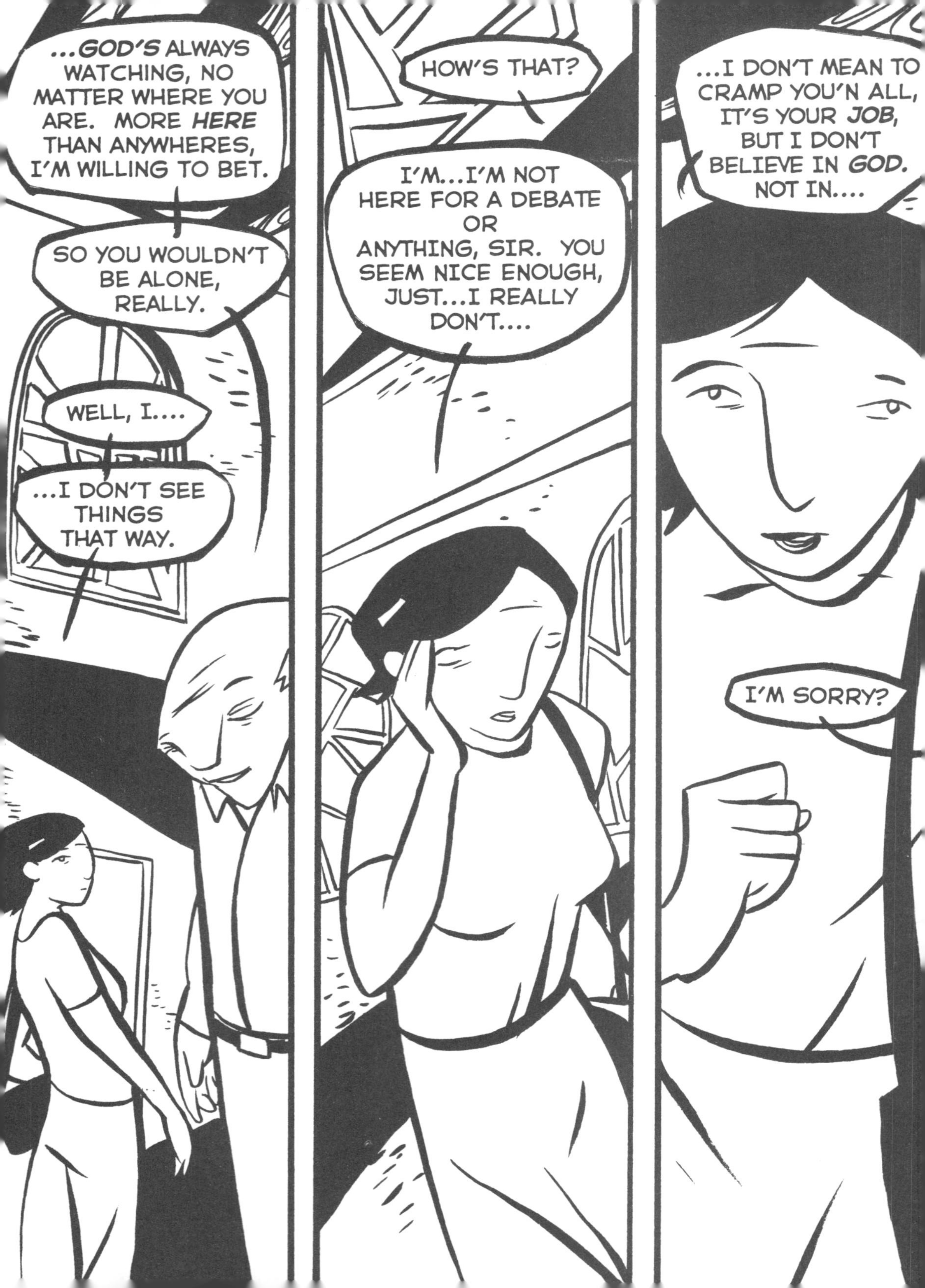
...GOD'S ALWAYS WATCHING, NO MATTER WHERE YOU ARE. MORE HERE THAN ANYWHERES, I'M WILLING TO BET.
SO YOU WOULDN'T BE ALONE, REALLY.
WELL, I....
...I DON'T SEE THINGS THAT WAY.
HOW'S THAT?
I'M...I'M NOT HERE FOR A DEBATE OR ANYTHING, SIR. YOU SEEM NICE ENOUGH, JUST...I REALLY DON'T....
...I DON'T MEAN TO CRAMP YOU'N ALL, IT'S YOUR JOB, BUT I DON'T BELIEVE IN GOD. NOT IN....
I'M SORRY?

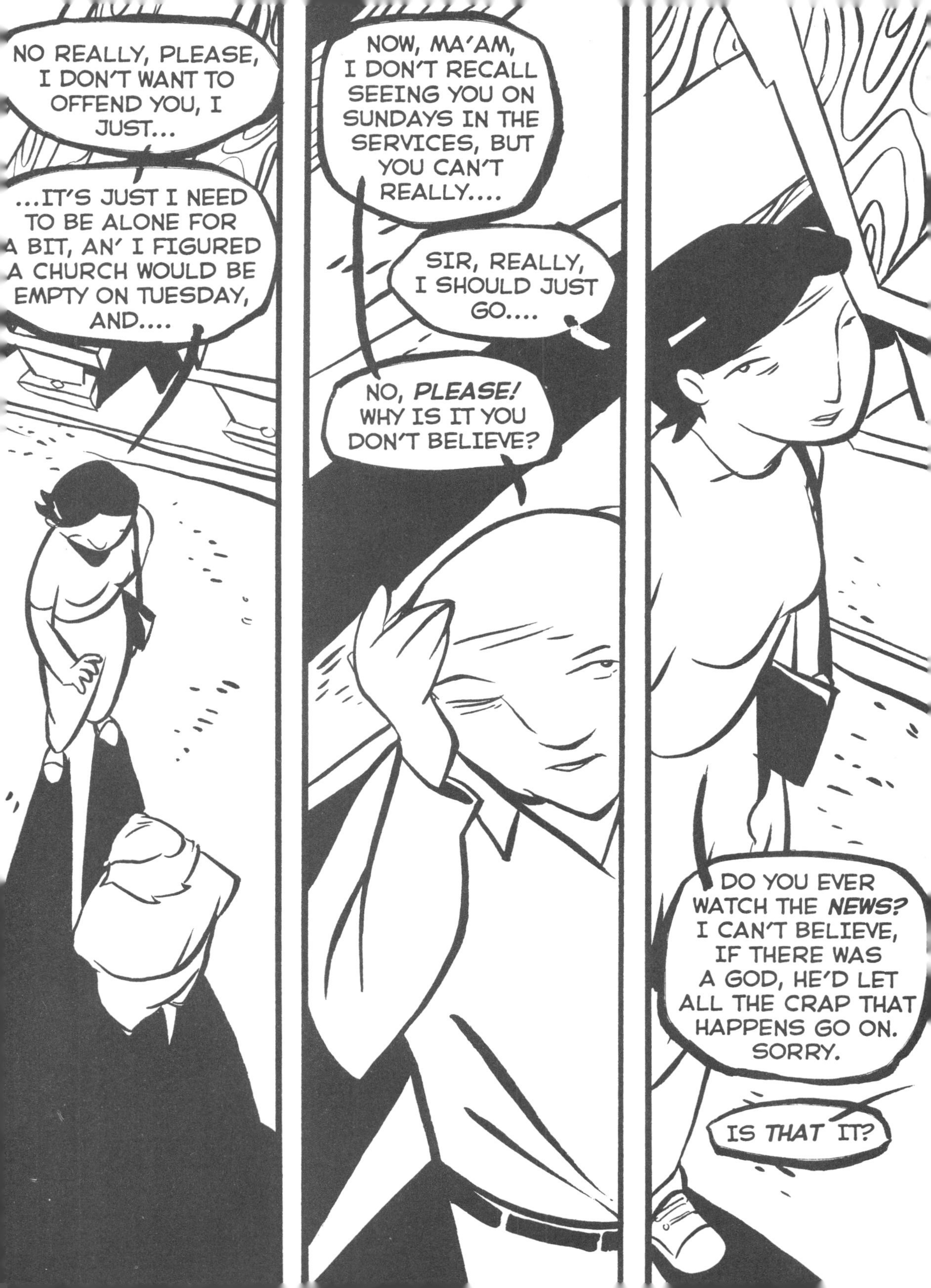
NO REALLY, PLEASE, I DON'T WANT TO OFFEND YOU, I JUST...
...IT'S JUST I NEED TO BE ALONE FOR A BIT, AN' I FIGURED A CHURCH WOULD BE EMPTY ON TUESDAY, AND....
NOW, MA'AM, I DON'T RECALL SEEING YOU ON SUNDAYS IN THE SERVICES, BUT YOU CAN'T REALLY....
SIR, REALLY, I SHOULD JUST GO....
NO, *PLEASE!* WHY IS IT YOU DON'T BELIEVE?
DO YOU EVER WATCH THE *NEWS?* I CAN'T BELIEVE, IF THERE WAS A GOD, HE'D LET ALL THE CRAP THAT HAPPENS GO ON. SORRY.
IS *THAT* IT?

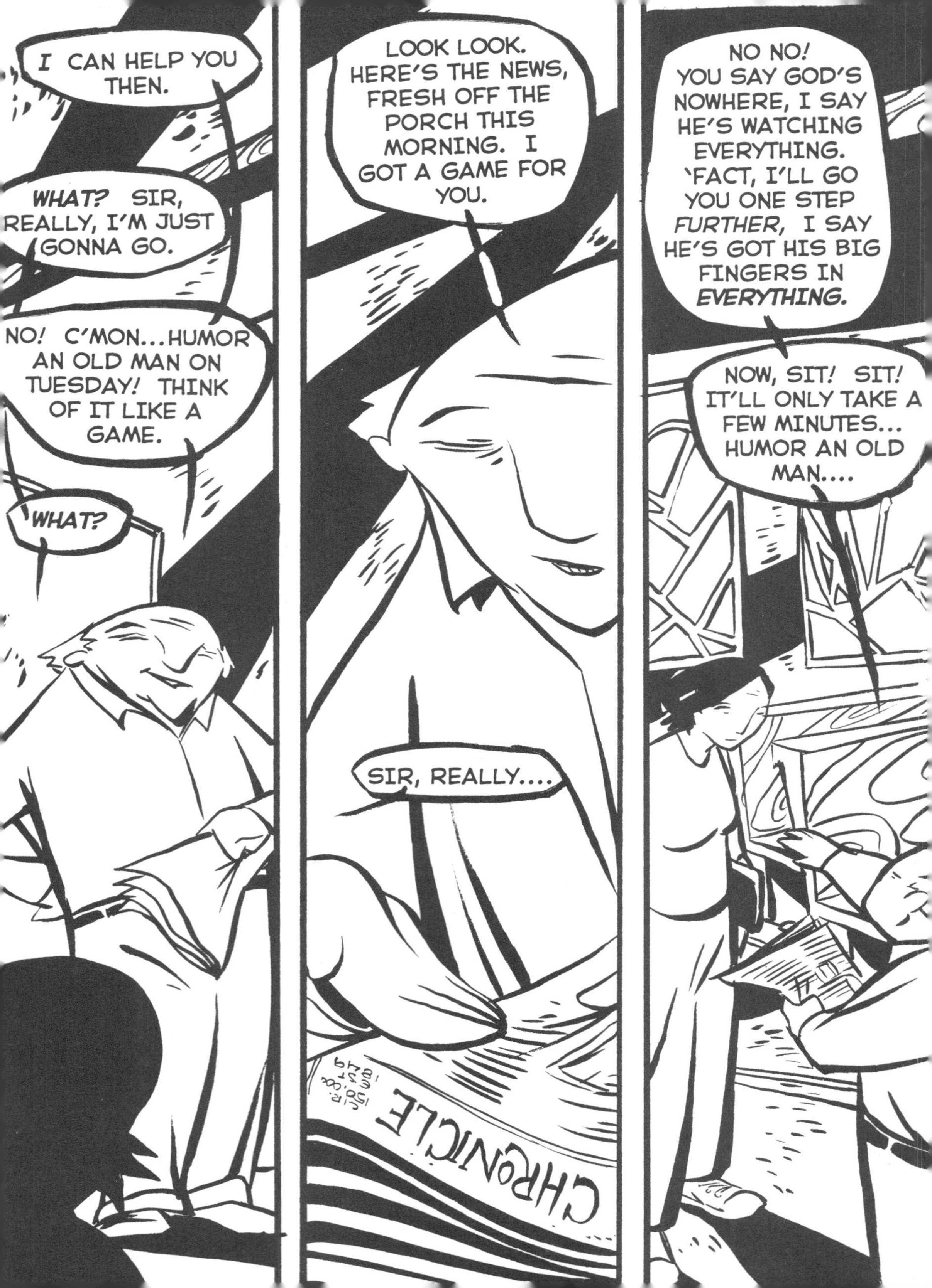
I CAN HELP YOU THEN.
WHAT? SIR, REALLY, I'M JUST GONNA GO.
NO! C'MON...HUMOR AN OLD MAN ON TUESDAY! THINK OF IT LIKE A GAME.
WHAT?
LOOK LOOK. HERE'S THE NEWS, FRESH OFF THE PORCH THIS MORNING. I GOT A GAME FOR YOU.
SIR, REALLY....
CHRONICLE
NO NO! YOU SAY GOD'S NOWHERE, I SAY HE'S WATCHING EVERYTHING. 'FACT, I'LL GO YOU ONE STEP *FURTHER,* I SAY HE'S GOT HIS BIG FINGERS IN *EVERYTHING.*
NOW, SIT! SIT! IT'LL ONLY TAKE A FEW MINUTES... HUMOR AN OLD MAN....

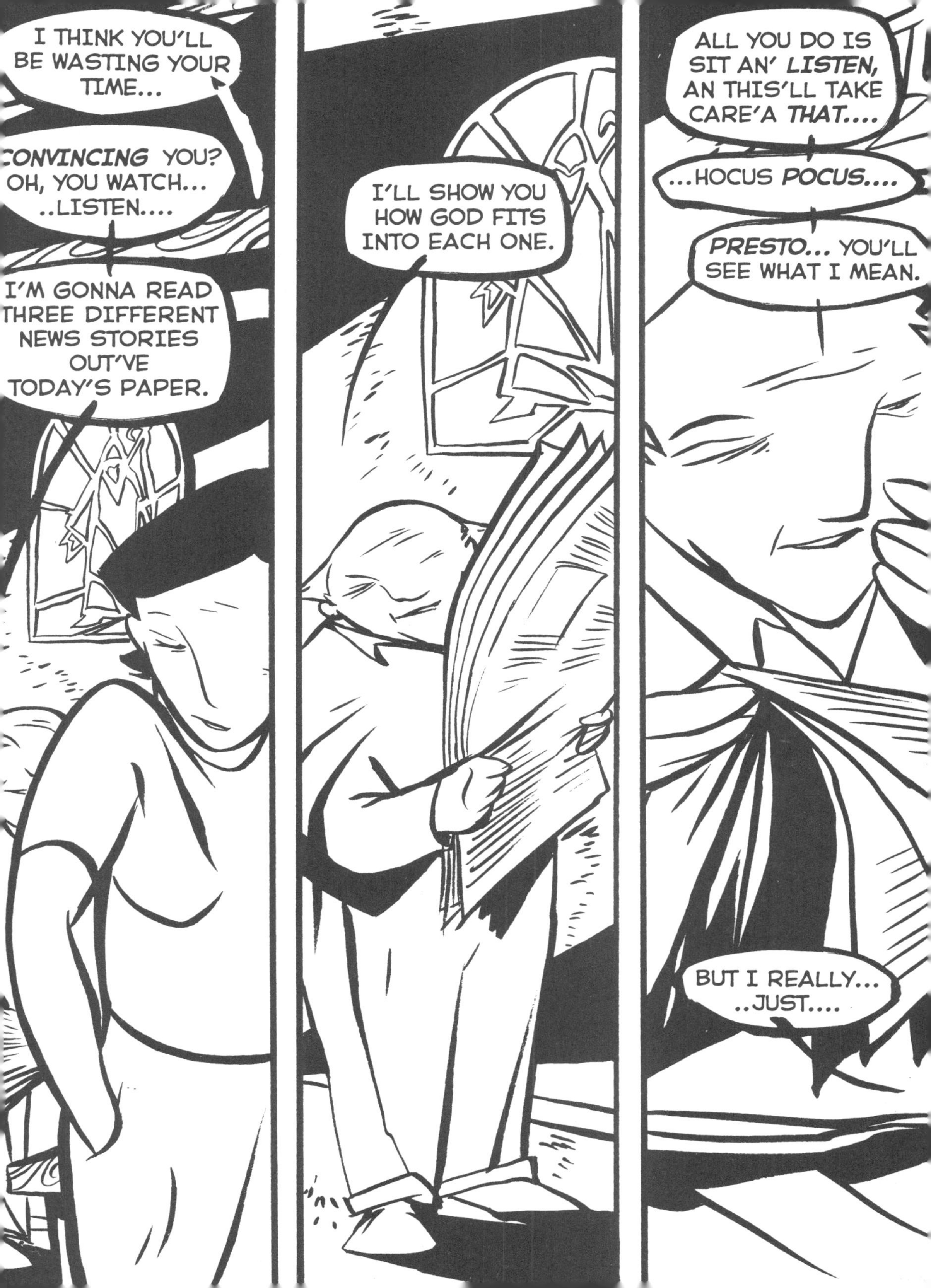
I THINK YOU'LL BE WASTING YOUR TIME...
CONVINCING YOU? OH, YOU WATCH... ..LISTEN....
I'M GONNA READ THREE DIFFERENT NEWS STORIES OUT'VE TODAY'S PAPER.
I'LL SHOW YOU HOW GOD FITS INTO EACH ONE.
ALL YOU DO IS SIT AN' LISTEN, AN THIS'LL TAKE CARE'A THAT....
...HOCUS POCUS....
PRESTO... YOU'LL SEE WHAT I MEAN.
BUT I REALLY... ..JUST....

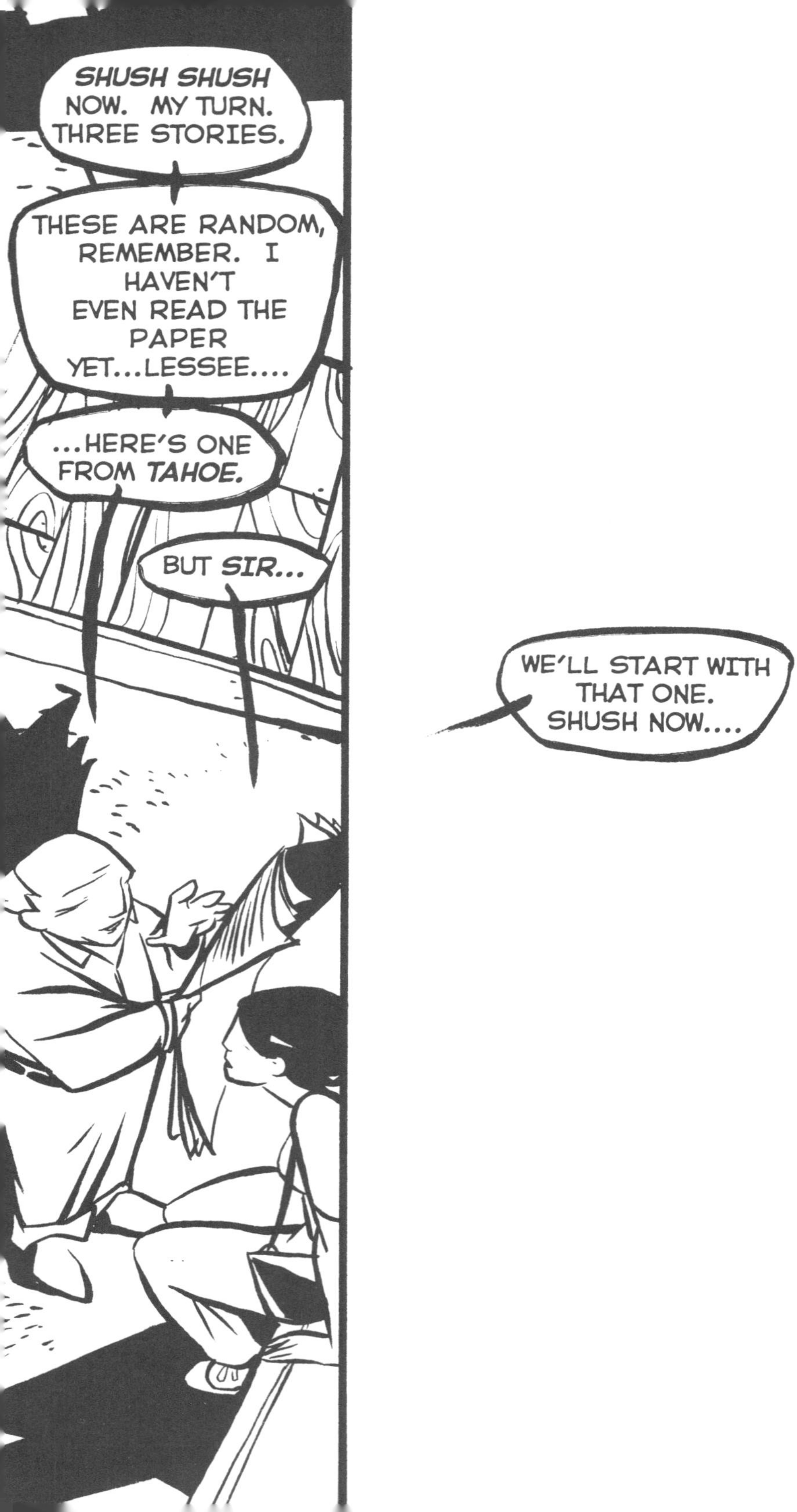
SHUSH SHUSH NOW. MY TURN. THREE STORIES.
THESE ARE RANDOM, REMEMBER. I HAVEN'T EVEN READ THE PAPER YET...LESSEE....
...HERE'S ONE FROM TAHOE.
BUT SIR...
WE'LL START WITH THAT ONE. SHUSH NOW....

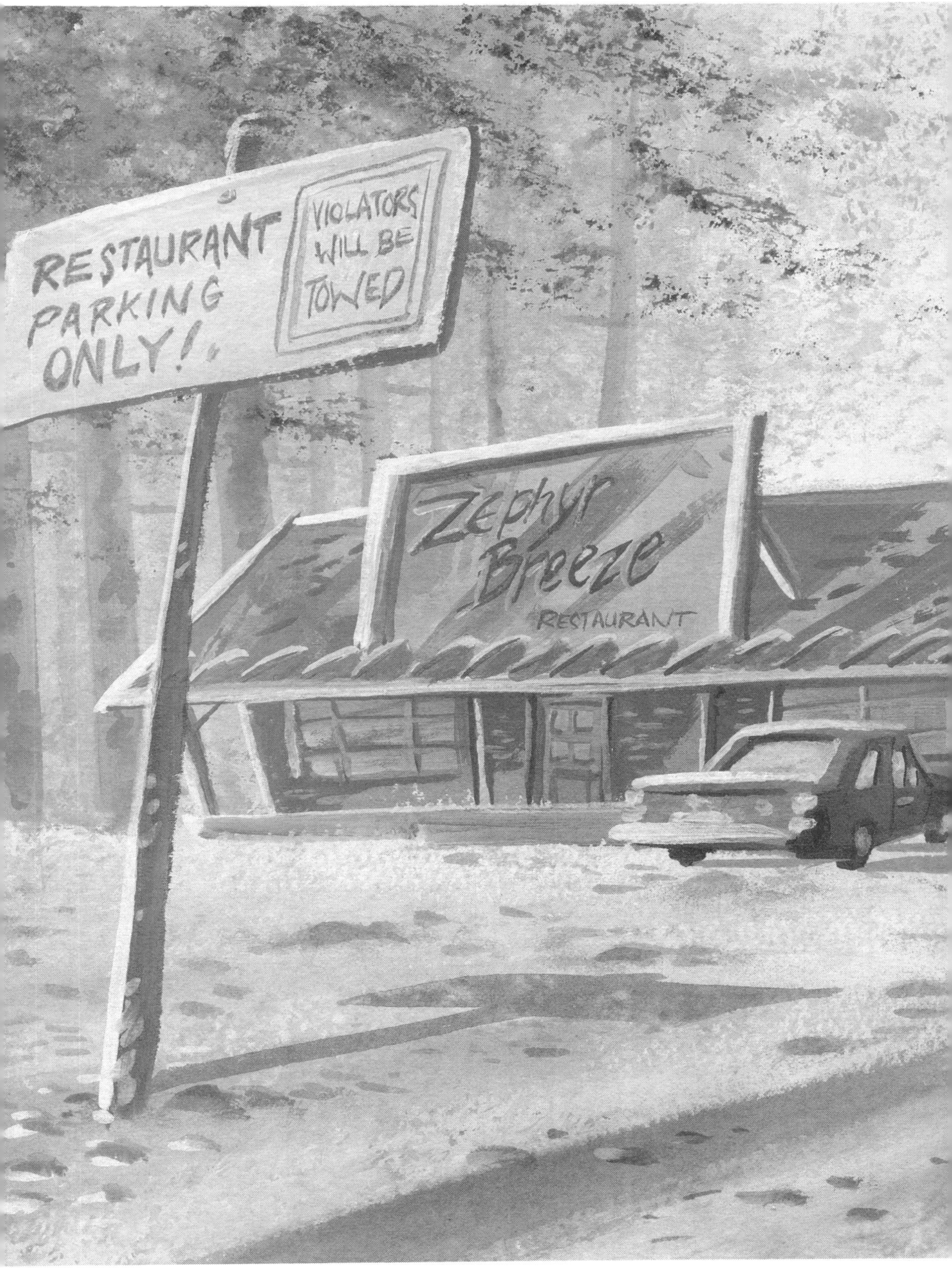
RESTAURANT PARKING ONLY!
VIOLATORS WILL BE TOWED
Zephyr Breeze
RESTAURANT

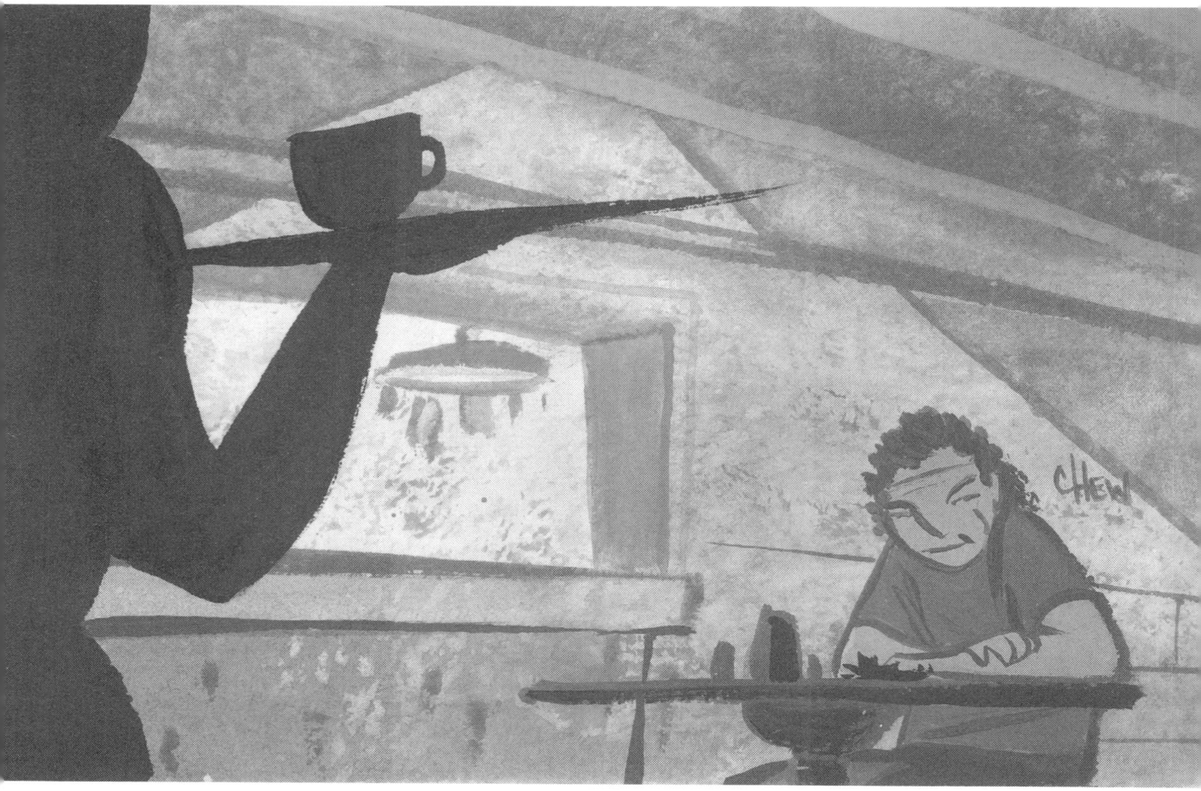
CHEW

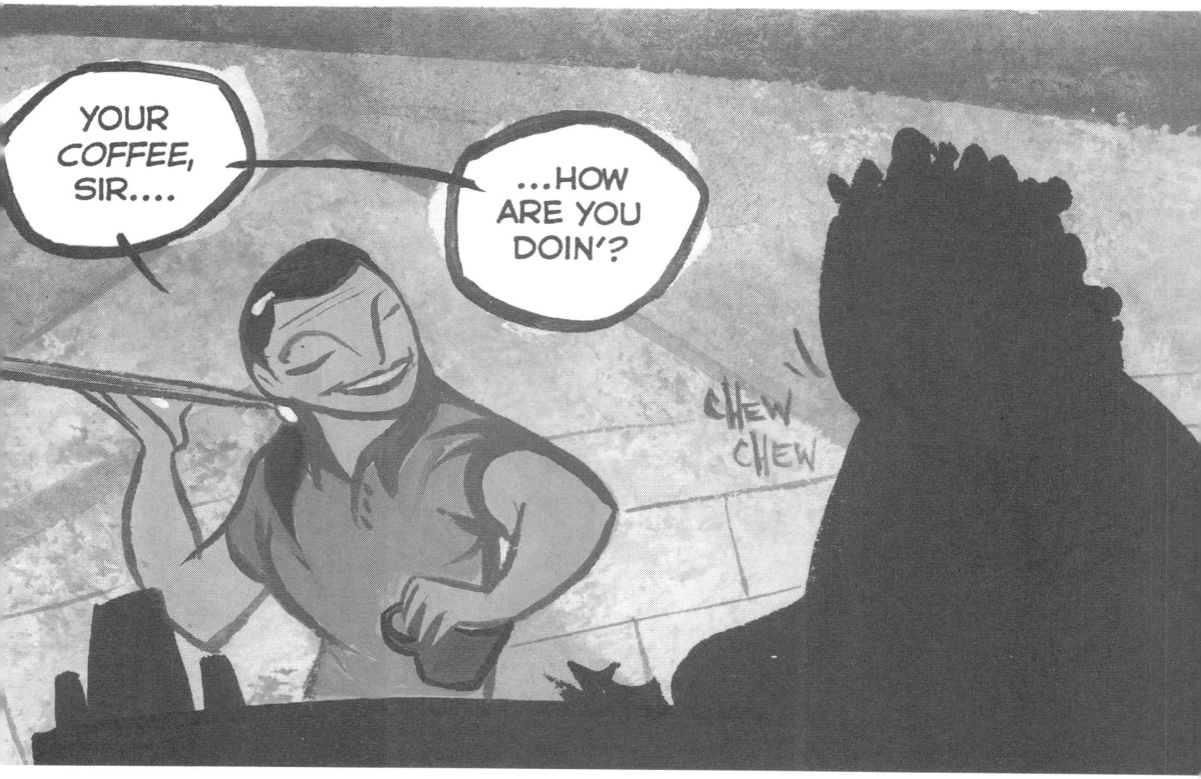
YOUR COFFEE, SIR....
...HOW ARE YOU DOIN'?
CHEW CHEW

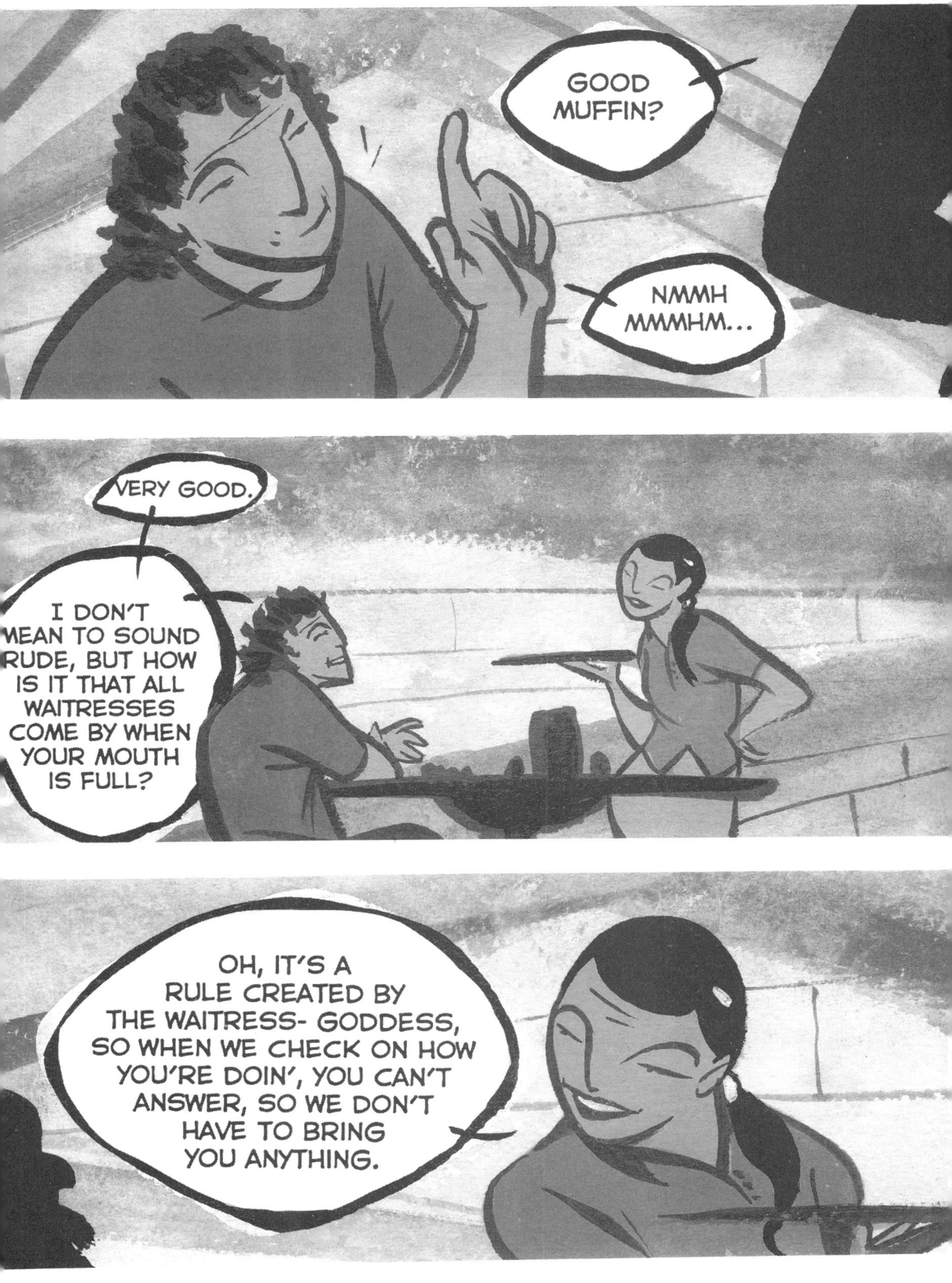
GOOD MUFFIN?
NMMH MMMHM...
VERY GOOD.
I DON'T MEAN TO SOUND RUDE, BUT HOW IS IT THAT ALL WAITRESSES COME BY WHEN YOUR MOUTH IS FULL?
OH, IT'S A RULE CREATED BY THE WAITRESS- GODDESS, SO WHEN WE CHECK ON HOW YOU'RE DOIN', YOU CAN'T ANSWER, SO WE DON'T HAVE TO BRING YOU ANYTHING.

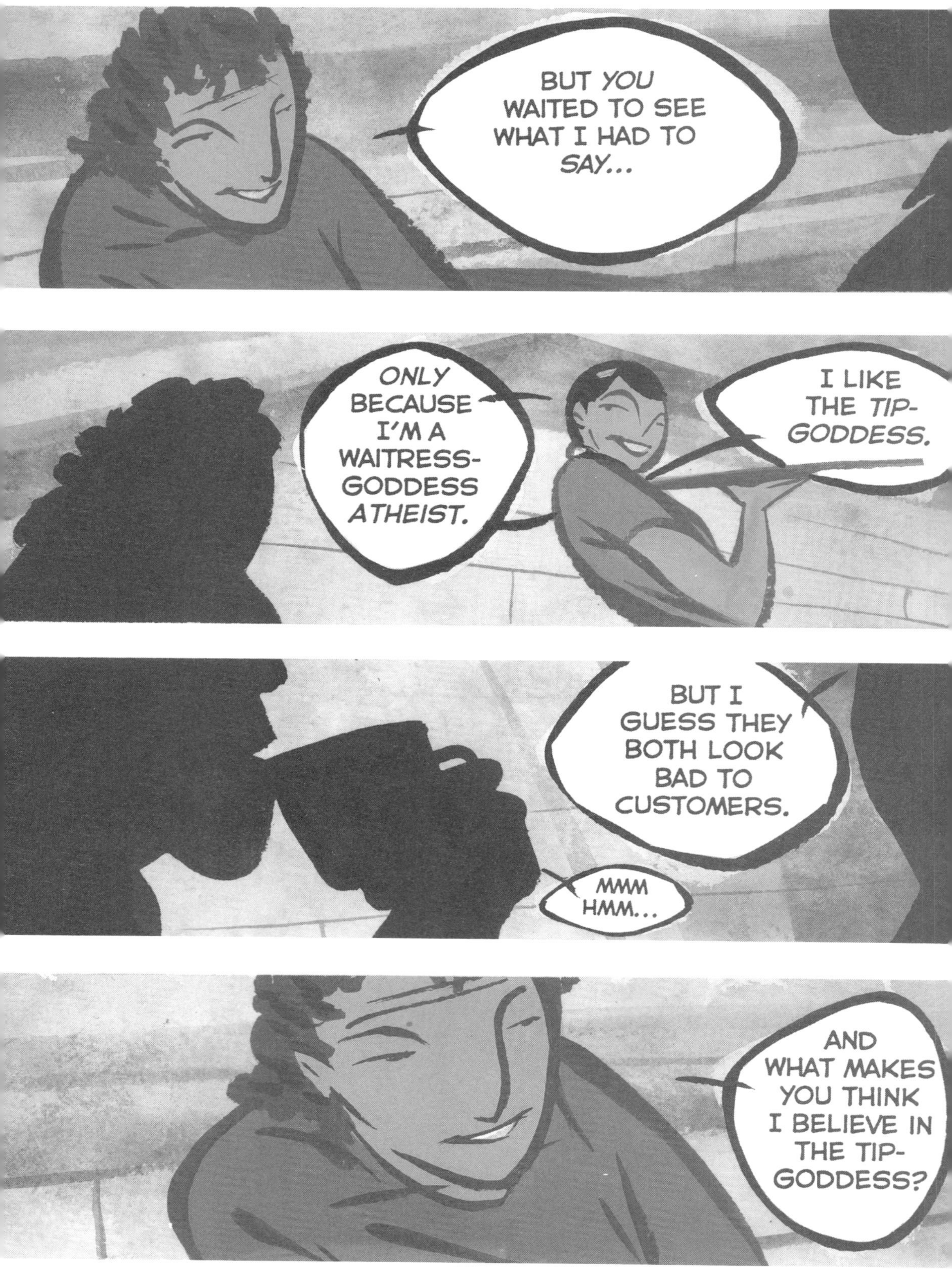
BUT *YOU* WAITED TO SEE WHAT I HAD TO *SAY*...
ONLY BECAUSE I'M A WAITRESS-GODDESS *ATHEIST.*
I LIKE THE *TIP-GODDESS.*
BUT I GUESS THEY BOTH LOOK BAD TO CUSTOMERS.
MMM HMM...
AND WHAT MAKES YOU THINK I BELIEVE IN THE TIP-GODDESS?

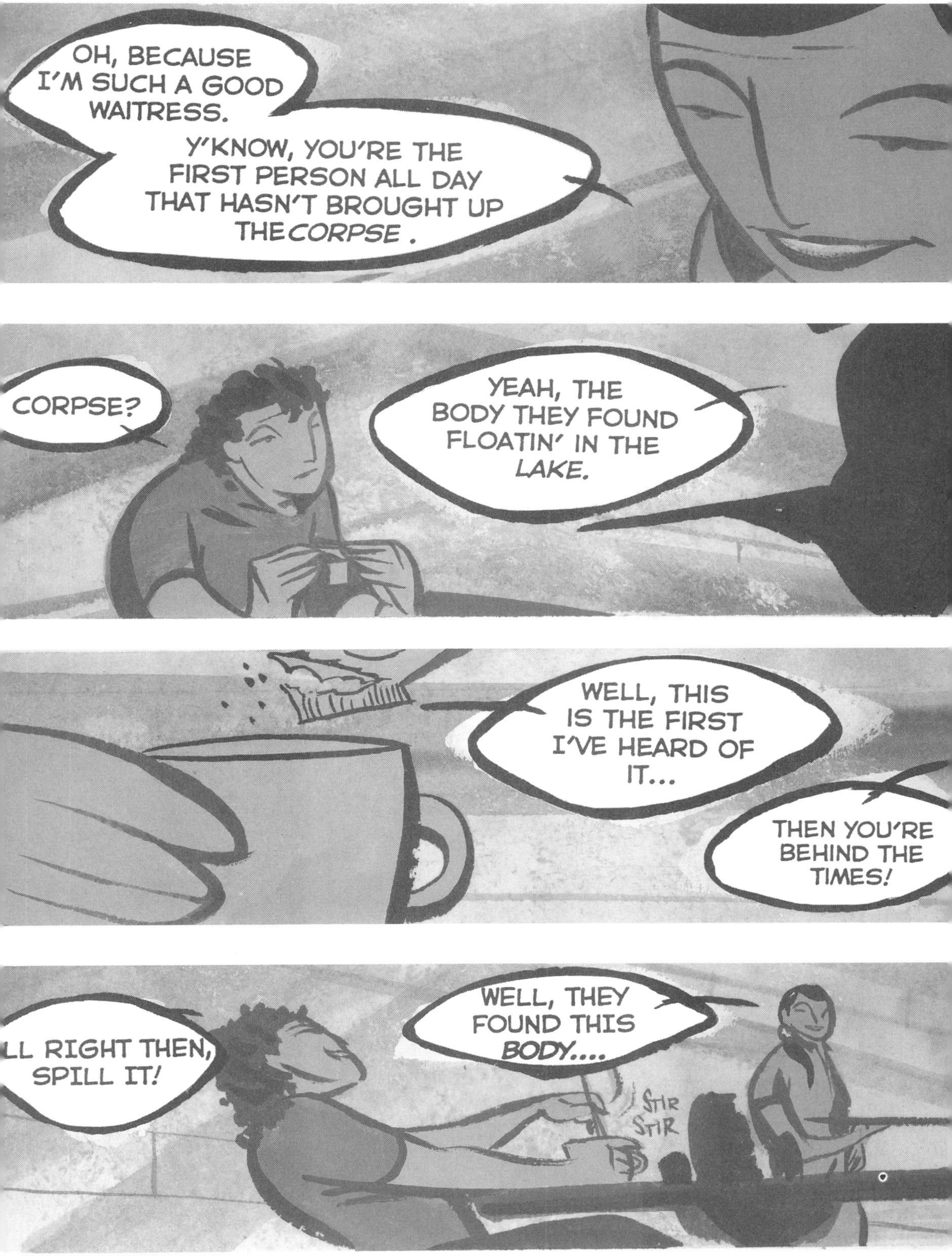

OH, BECAUSE I'M SUCH A GOOD WAITRESS.
Y'KNOW, YOU'RE THE FIRST PERSON ALL DAY THAT HASN'T BROUGHT UP THE *CORPSE* .
CORPSE?
YEAH, THE BODY THEY FOUND FLOATIN' IN THE *LAKE.*
WELL, THIS IS THE FIRST I'VE HEARD OF IT...
THEN YOU'RE BEHIND THE TIMES!
LL RIGHT THEN, SPILL IT!
WELL, THEY FOUND THIS *BODY....*
STIR
STIR

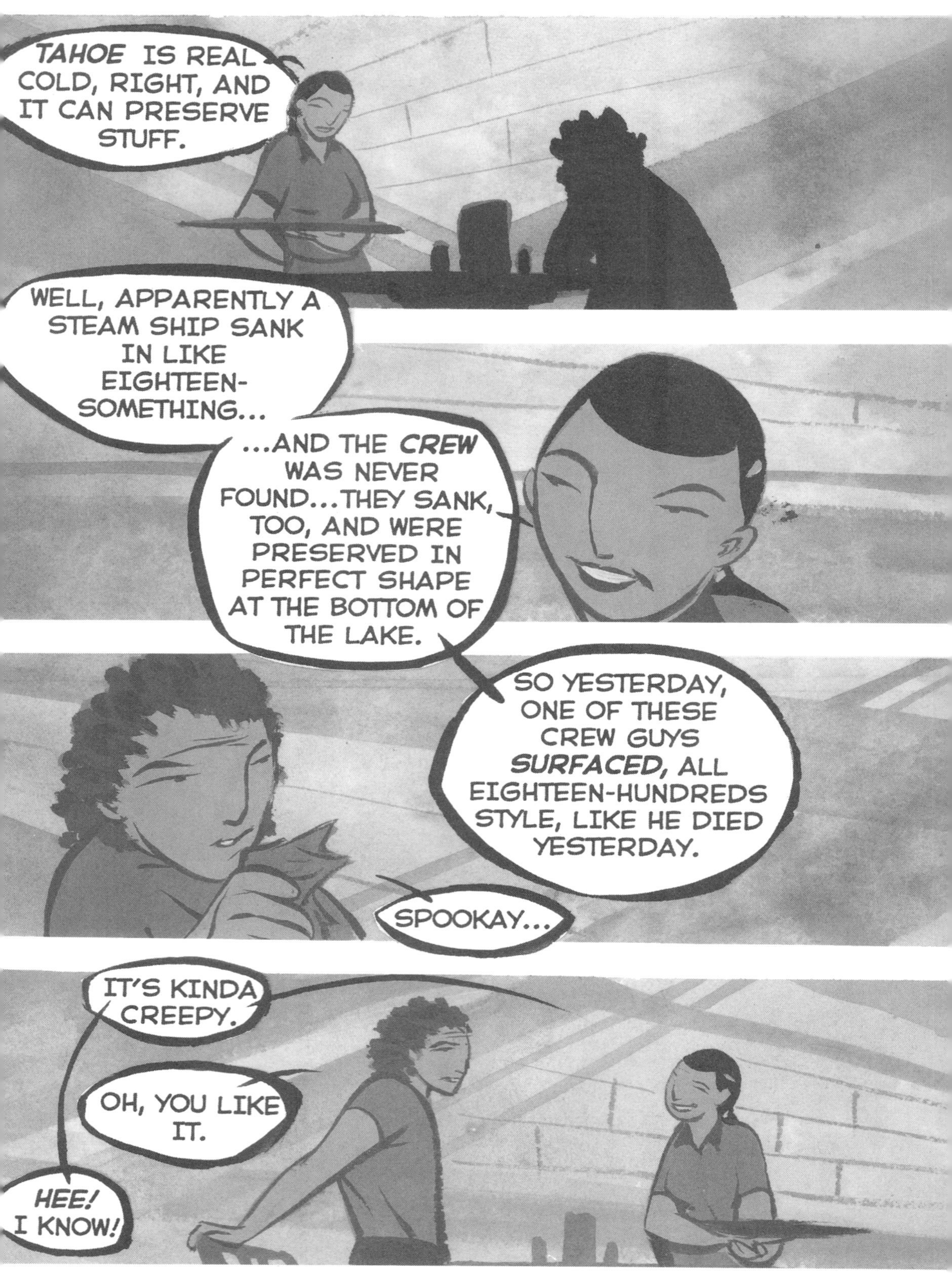
TAHOE IS REAL COLD, RIGHT, AND IT CAN PRESERVE STUFF.
WELL, APPARENTLY A STEAM SHIP SANK IN LIKE EIGHTEEN-SOMETHING...
...AND THE CREW WAS NEVER FOUND...THEY SANK, TOO, AND WERE PRESERVED IN PERFECT SHAPE AT THE BOTTOM OF THE LAKE.
SO YESTERDAY, ONE OF THESE CREW GUYS SURFACED, ALL EIGHTEEN-HUNDREDS STYLE, LIKE HE DIED YESTERDAY.
SPOOKAY...
IT'S KINDA CREEPY.
OH, YOU LIKE IT.
HEE! I KNOW!

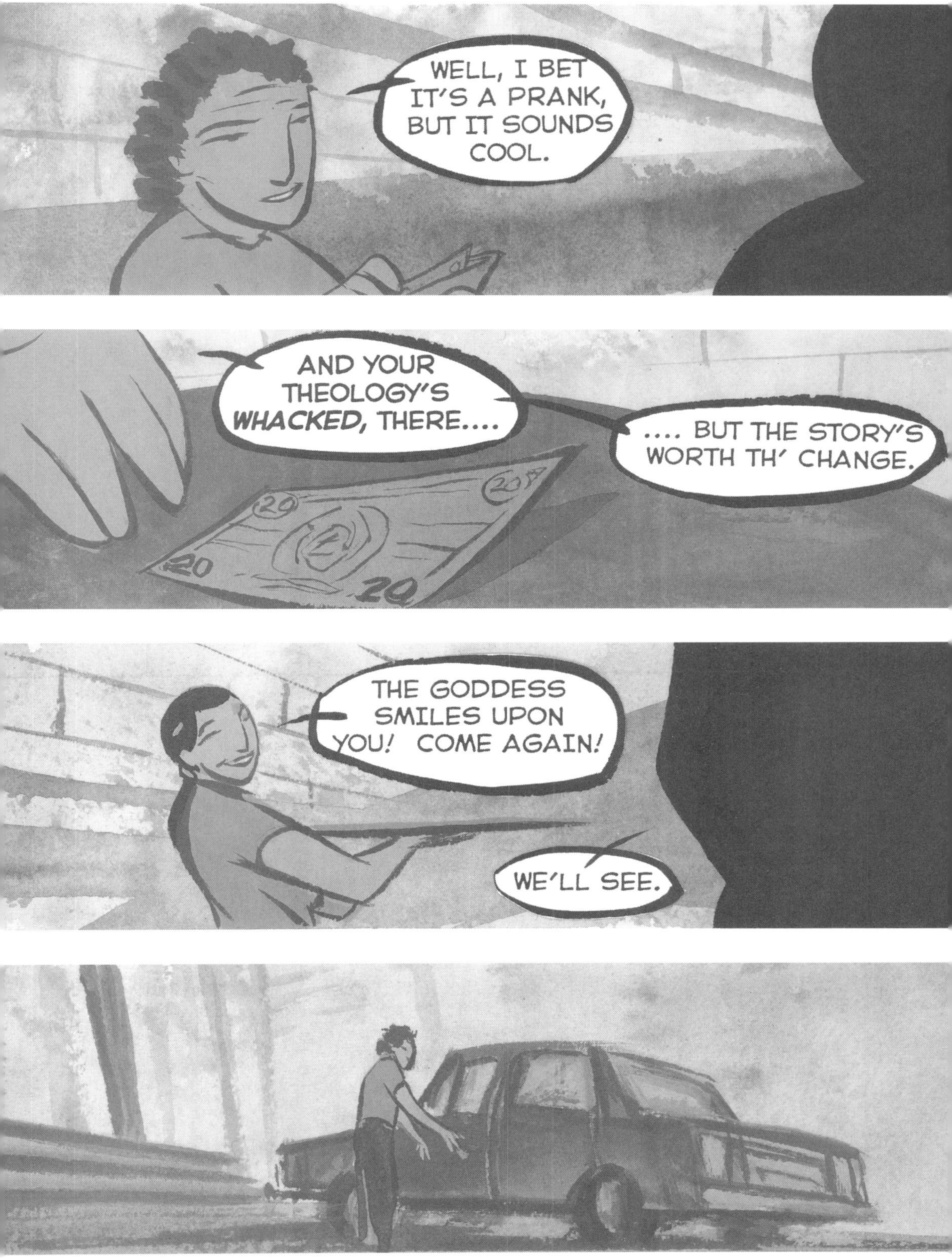
WELL, I BET IT'S A PRANK, BUT IT SOUNDS COOL.
AND YOUR THEOLOGY'S *WHACKED*, THERE....
.... BUT THE STORY'S WORTH TH' CHANGE.
THE GODDESS SMILES UPON YOU! COME AGAIN!
WE'LL SEE.

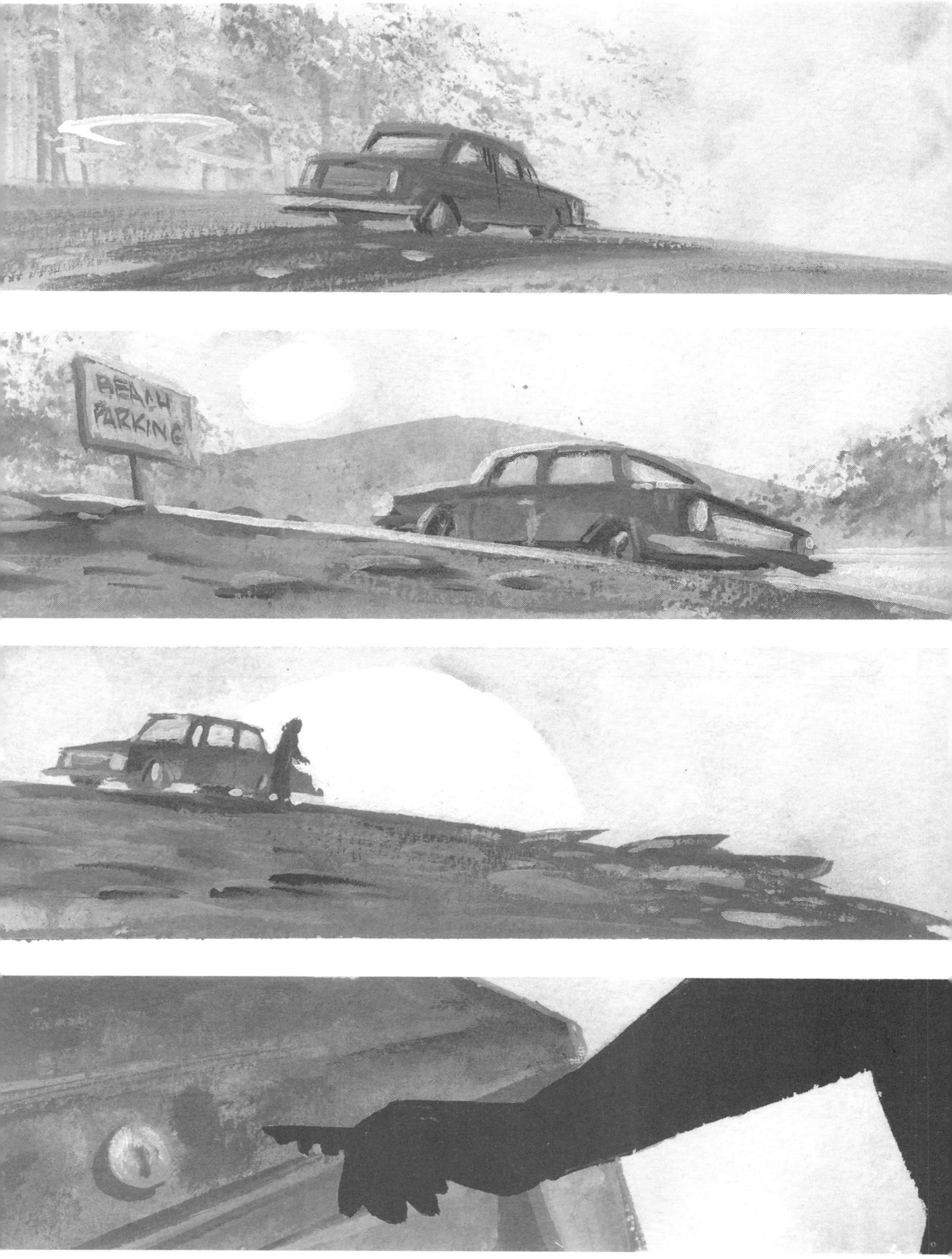
BEACH PARKING

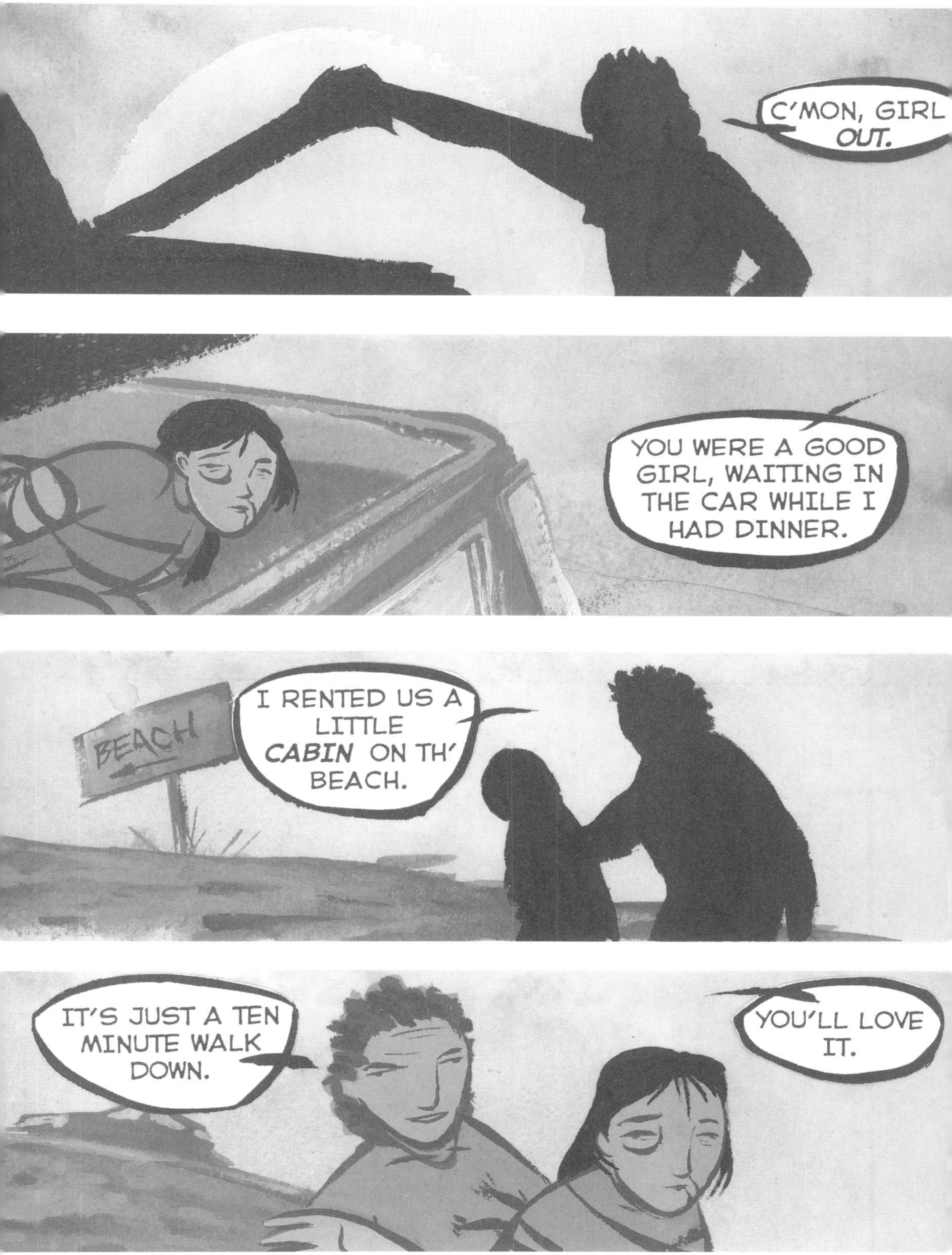
C'MON, GIRL
OUT.
YOU WERE A GOOD GIRL, WAITING IN THE CAR WHILE I HAD DINNER.
BEACH
I RENTED US A LITTLE CABIN ON TH' BEACH.
IT'S JUST A TEN MINUTE WALK DOWN.
YOU'LL LOVE IT.

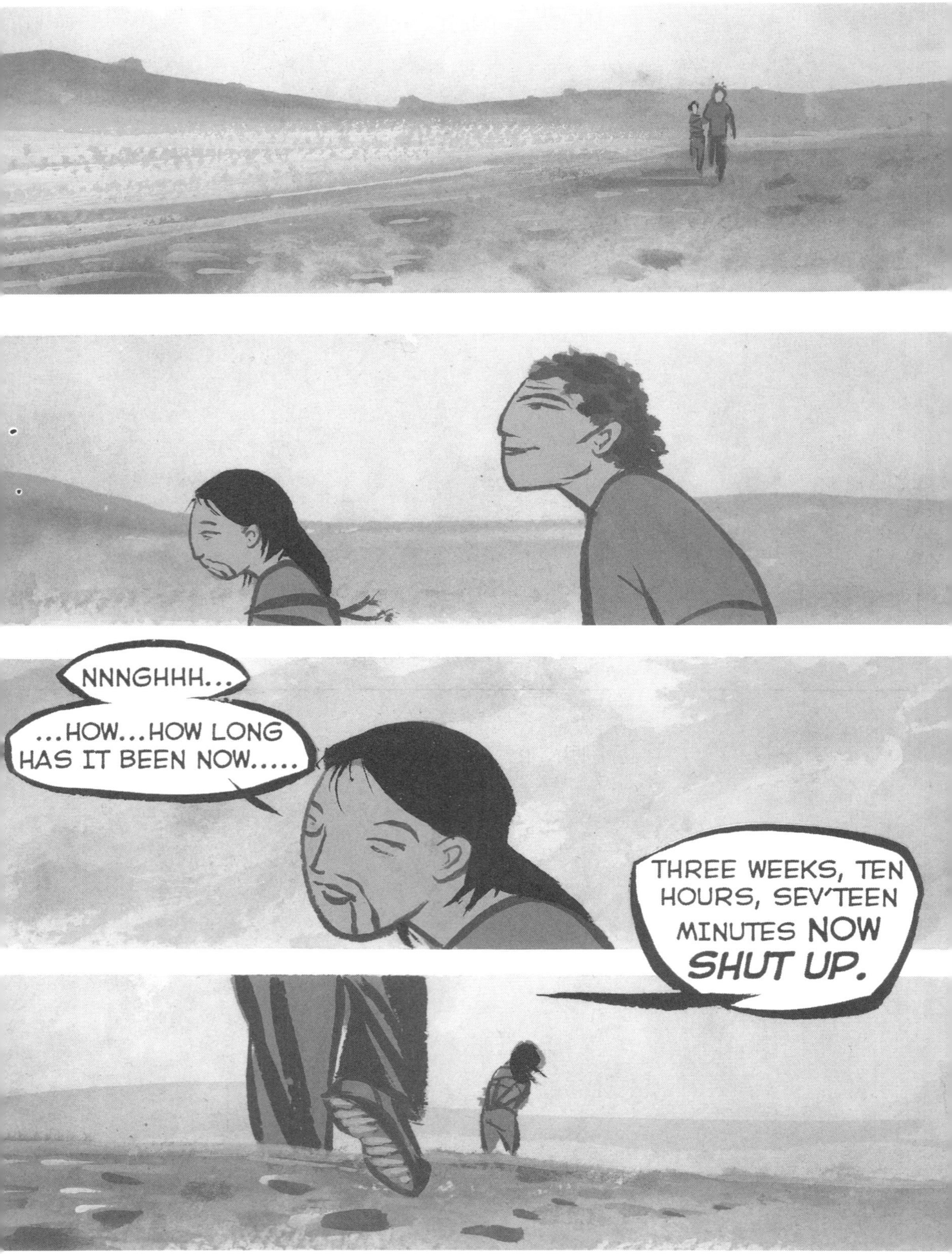
NNNGHHH...
...HOW...HOW LONG HAS IT BEEN NOW.....
THREE WEEKS, TEN HOURS, SEV'TEEN MINUTES NOW SHUT UP.

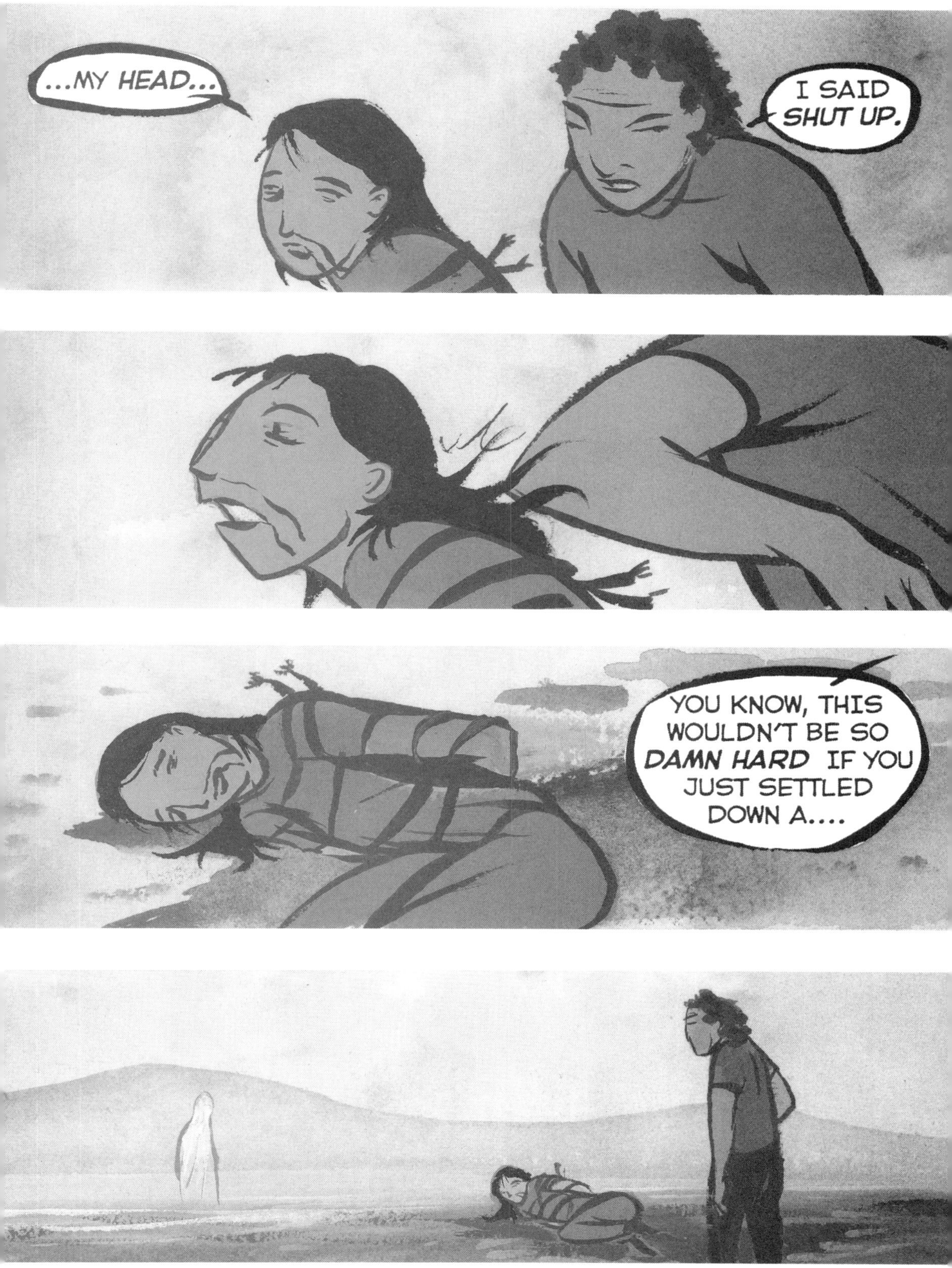
...MY HEAD...
I SAID SHUT UP.
YOU KNOW, THIS WOULDN'T BE SO DAMN HARD IF YOU JUST SETTLED DOWN A....

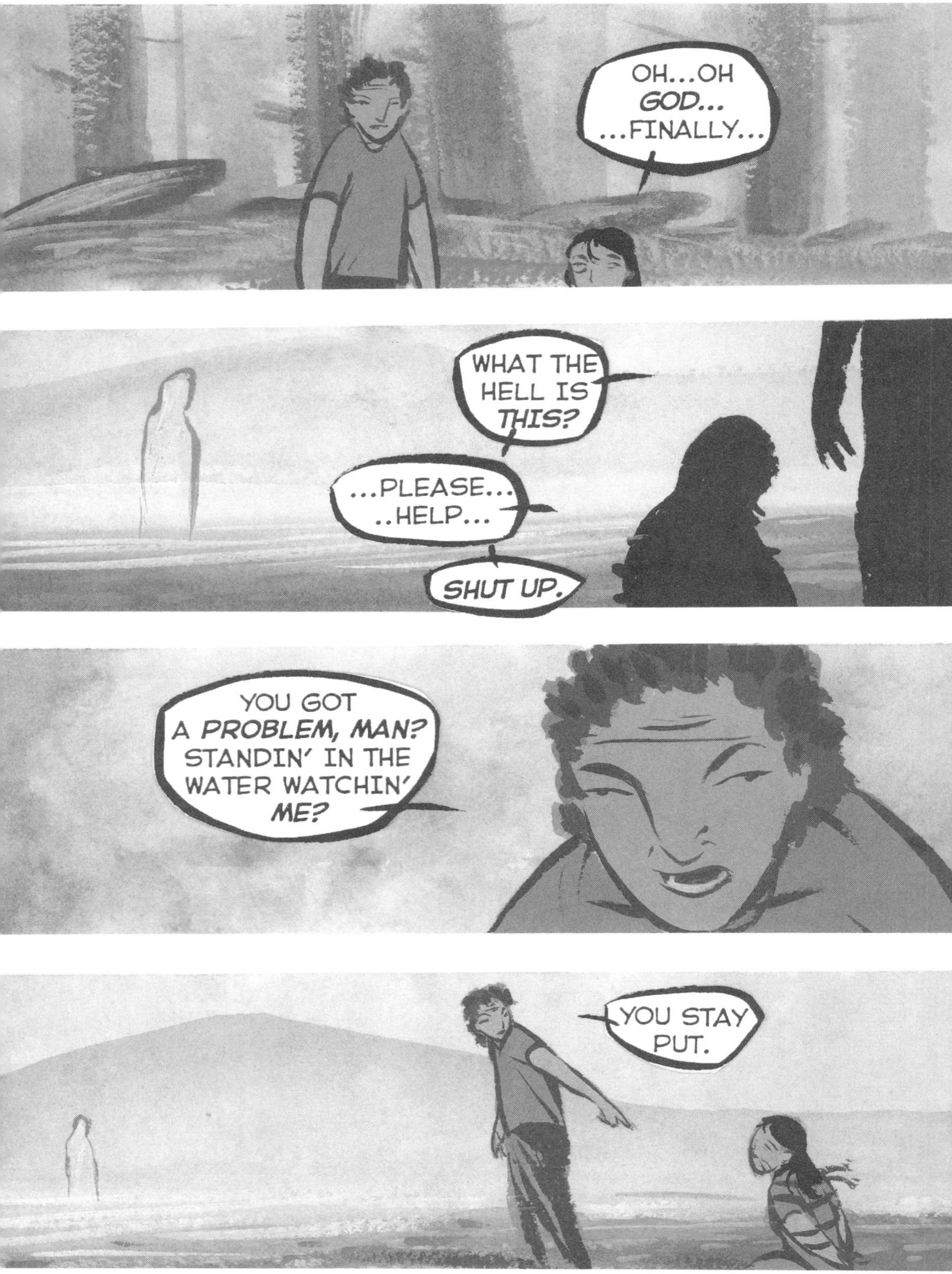
OH...OH GOD... ...FINALLY...
WHAT THE HELL IS THIS?
...PLEASE... ..HELP...
SHUT UP.
YOU GOT A PROBLEM, MAN? STANDIN' IN THE WATER WATCHIN' ME?
YOU STAY PUT.

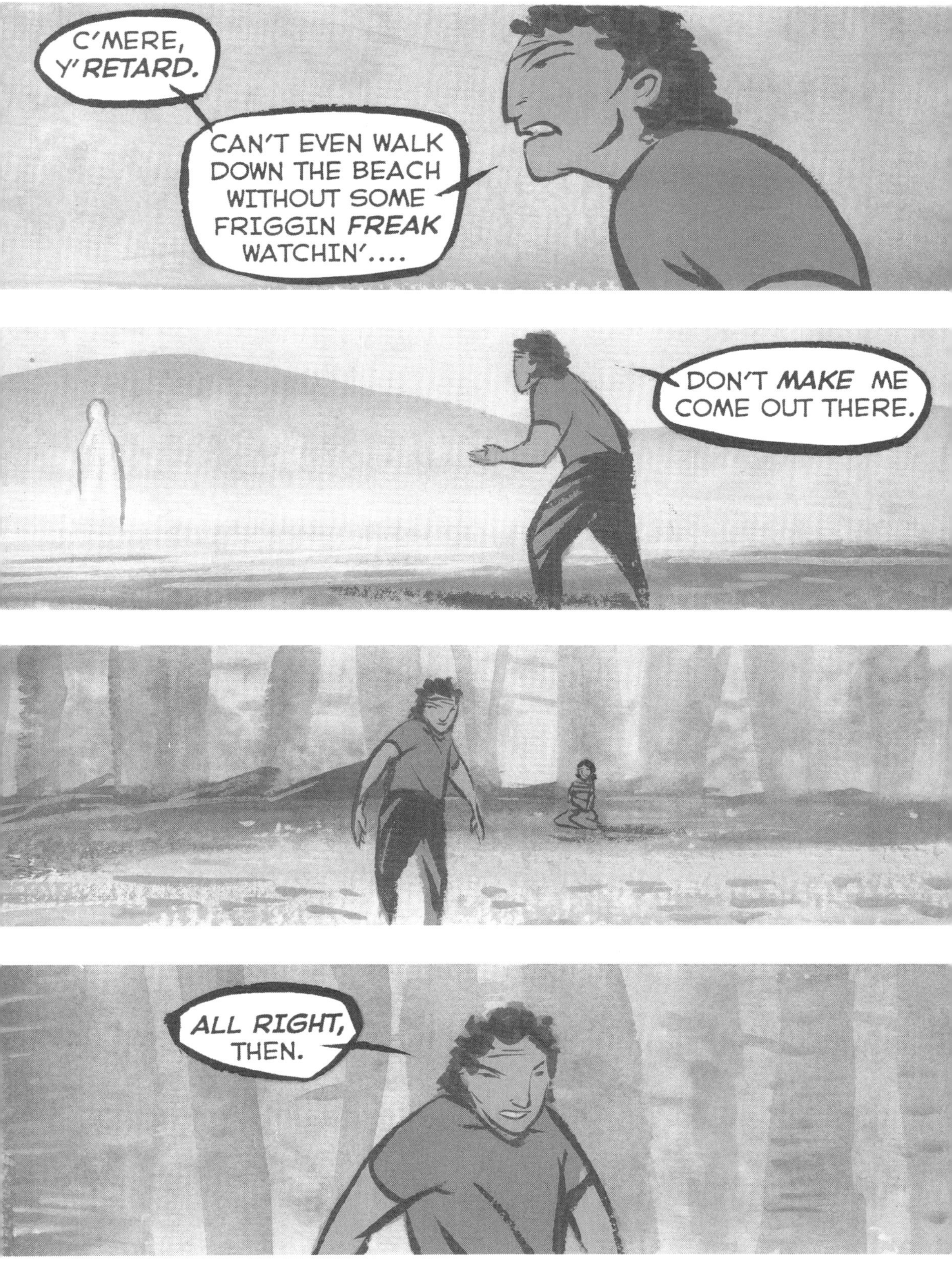
C'MERE, Y' RETARD.
CAN'T EVEN WALK DOWN THE BEACH WITHOUT SOME FRIGGIN FREAK WATCHIN'....
DON'T MAKE ME COME OUT THERE.
ALL RIGHT, THEN.

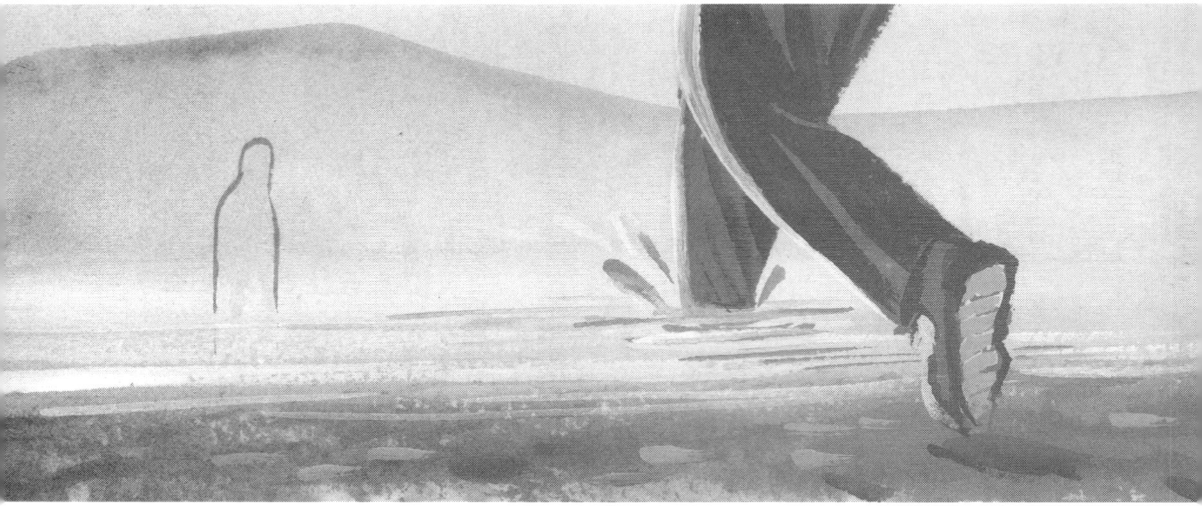

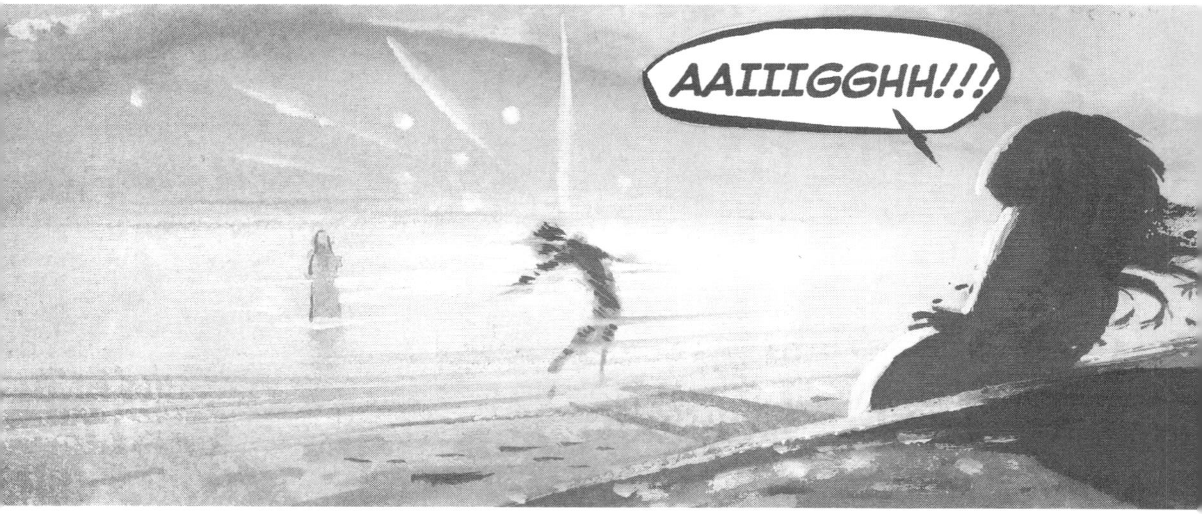
AAIIIGGHH!!!

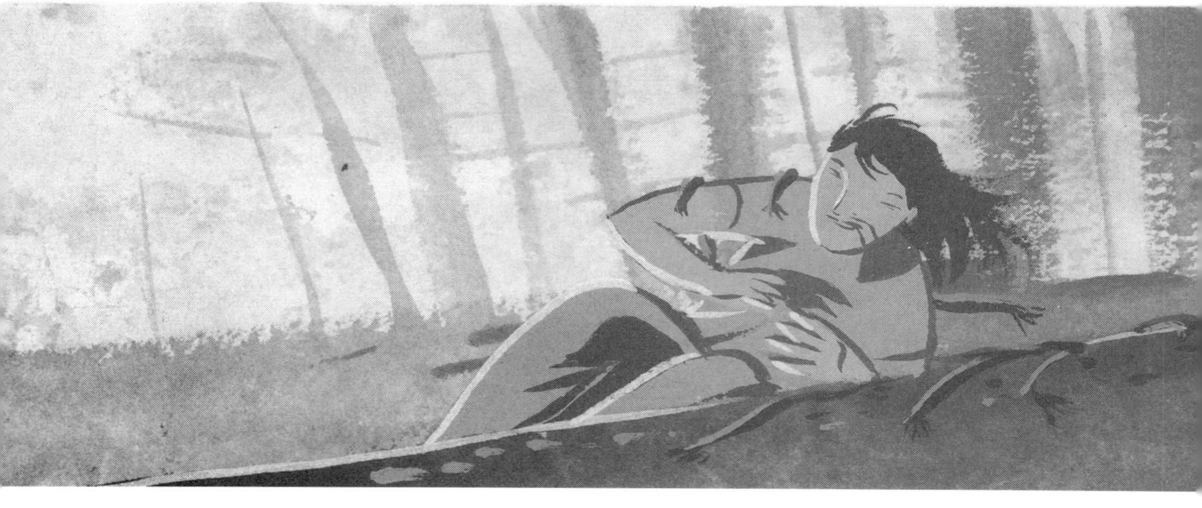

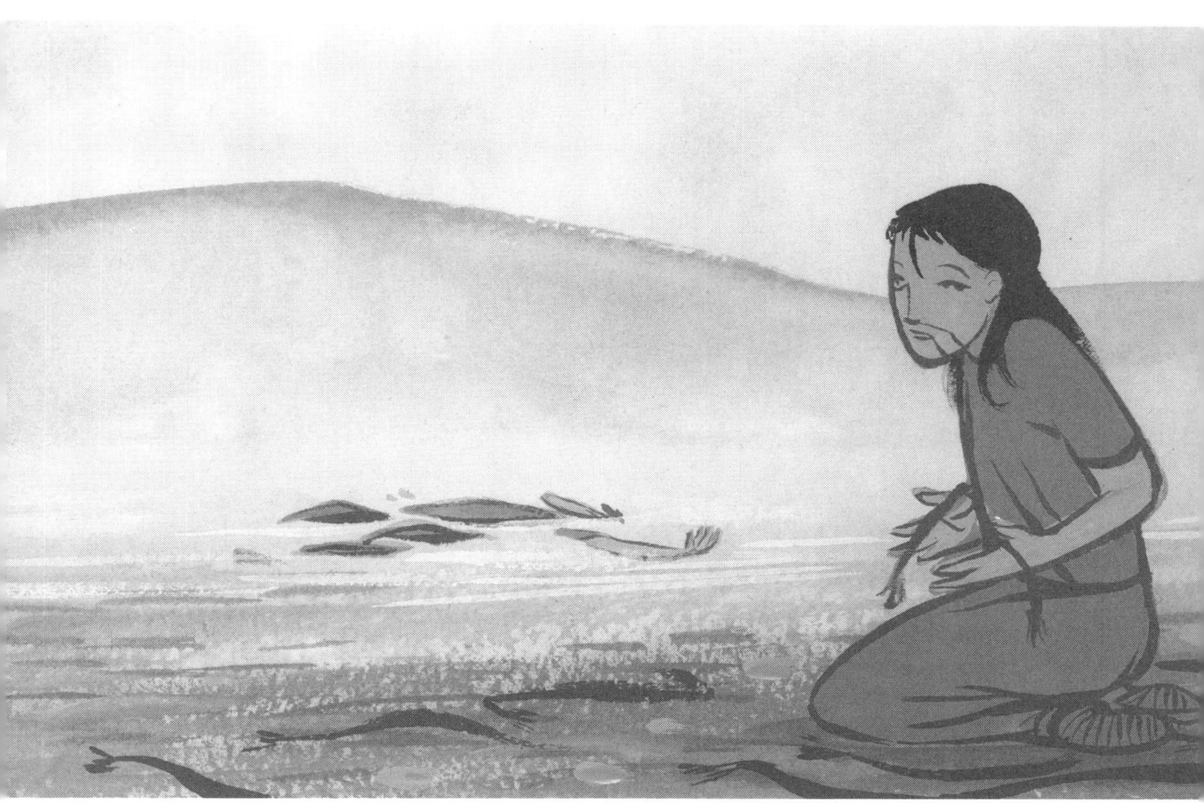

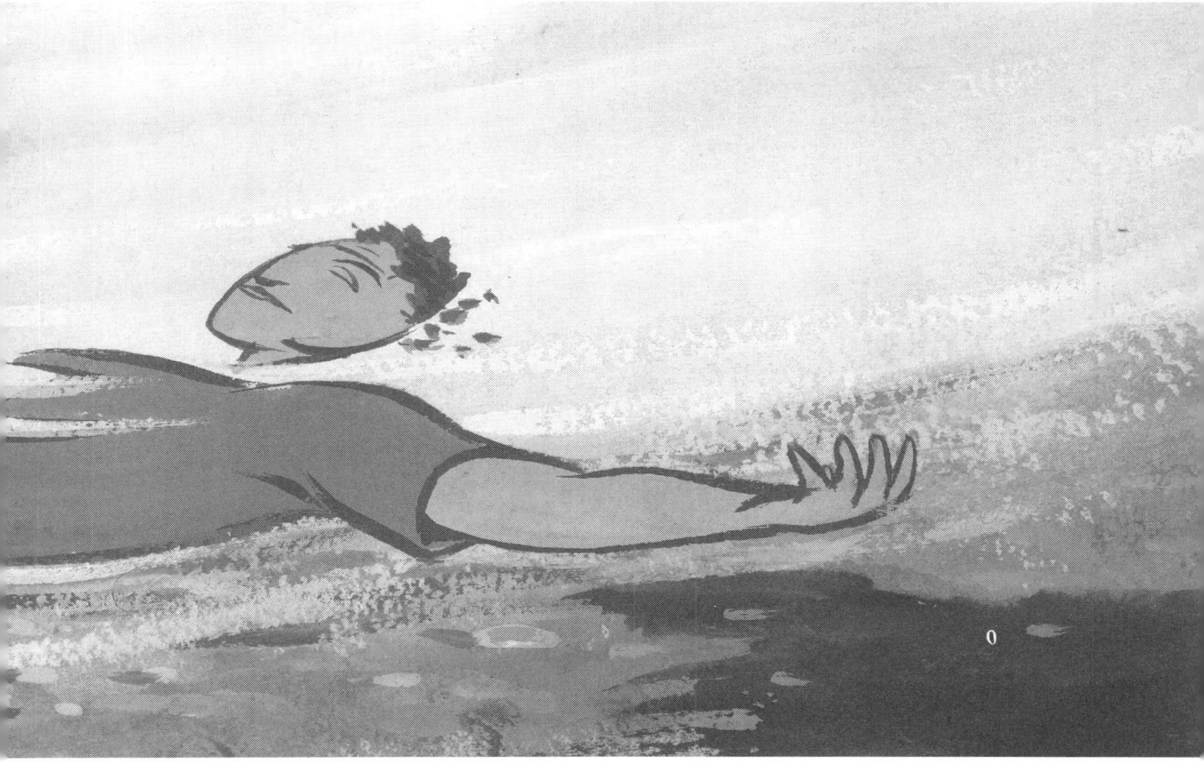

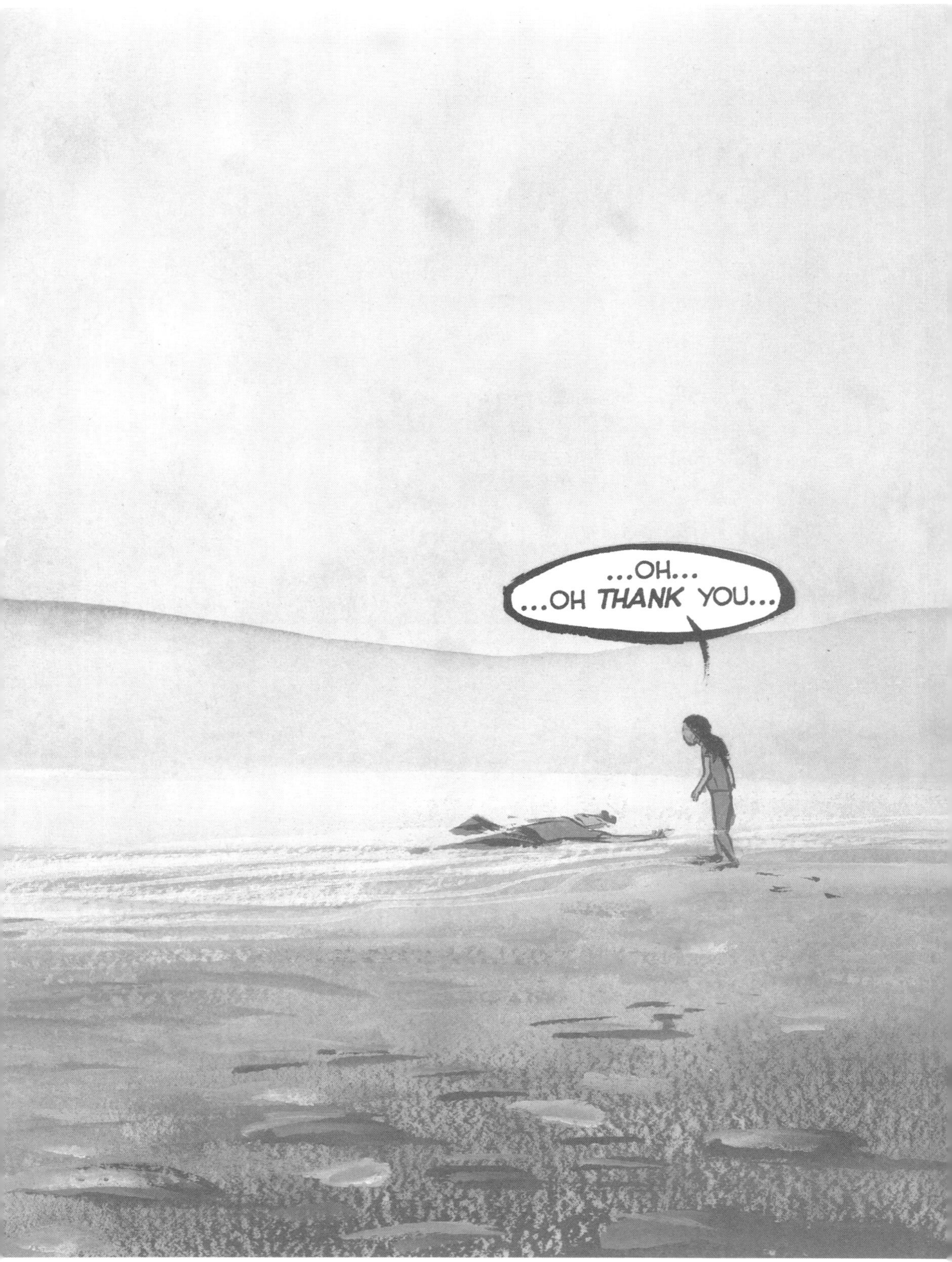
...OH...
...OH THANK YOU...

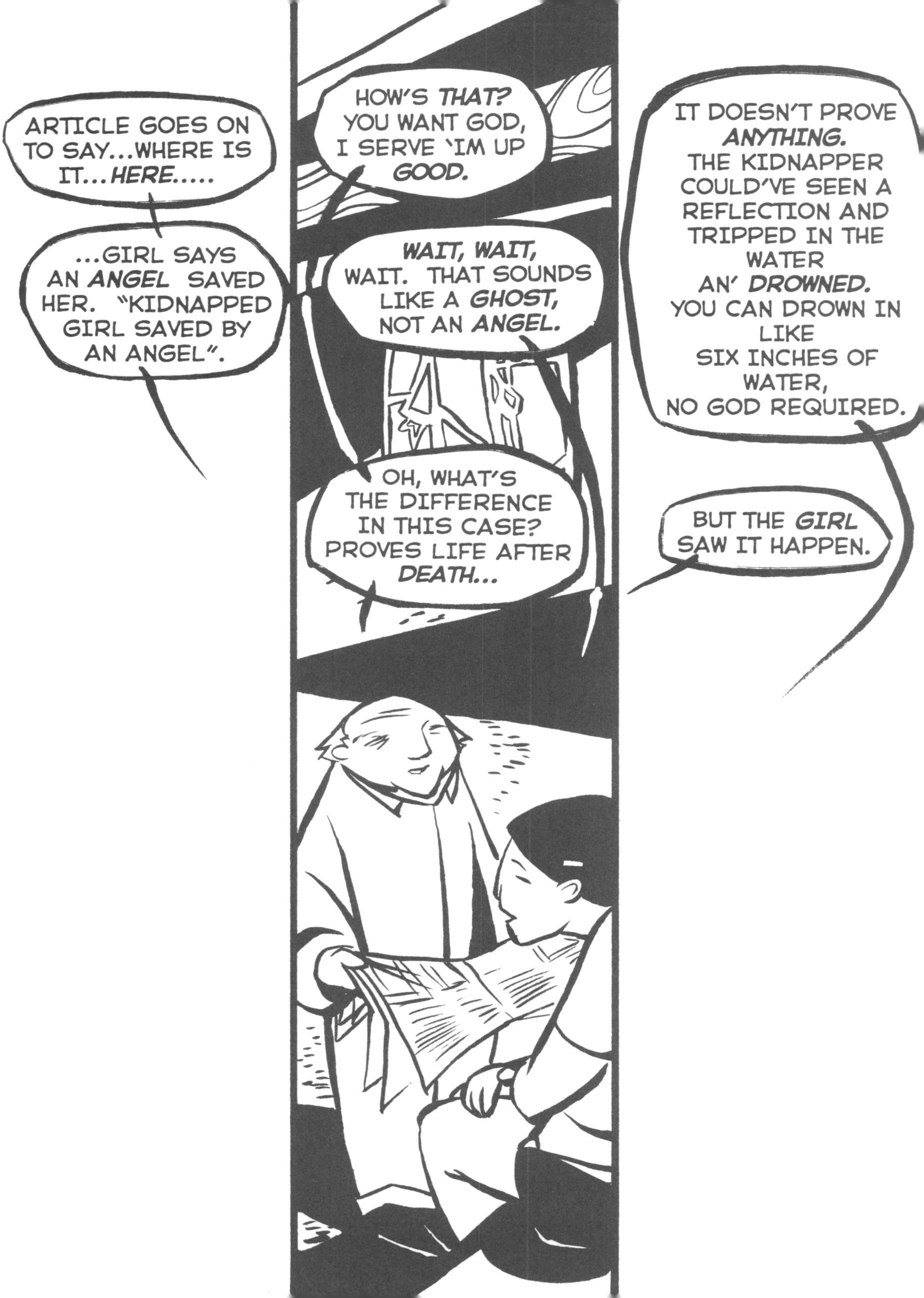
ARTICLE GOES ON TO SAY...WHERE IS IT...HERE.....
...GIRL SAYS AN ANGEL SAVED HER. "KIDNAPPED GIRL SAVED BY AN ANGEL".
HOW'S THAT? YOU WANT GOD, I SERVE 'IM UP GOOD.
WAIT, WAIT, WAIT. THAT SOUNDS LIKE A GHOST, NOT AN ANGEL.
OH, WHAT'S THE DIFFERENCE IN THIS CASE? PROVES LIFE AFTER DEATH...
IT DOESN'T PROVE ANYTHING. THE KIDNAPPER COULD'VE SEEN A REFLECTION AND TRIPPED IN THE WATER AN' DROWNED. YOU CAN DROWN IN LIKE SIX INCHES OF WATER, NO GOD REQUIRED.
BUT THE GIRL SAW IT HAPPEN.

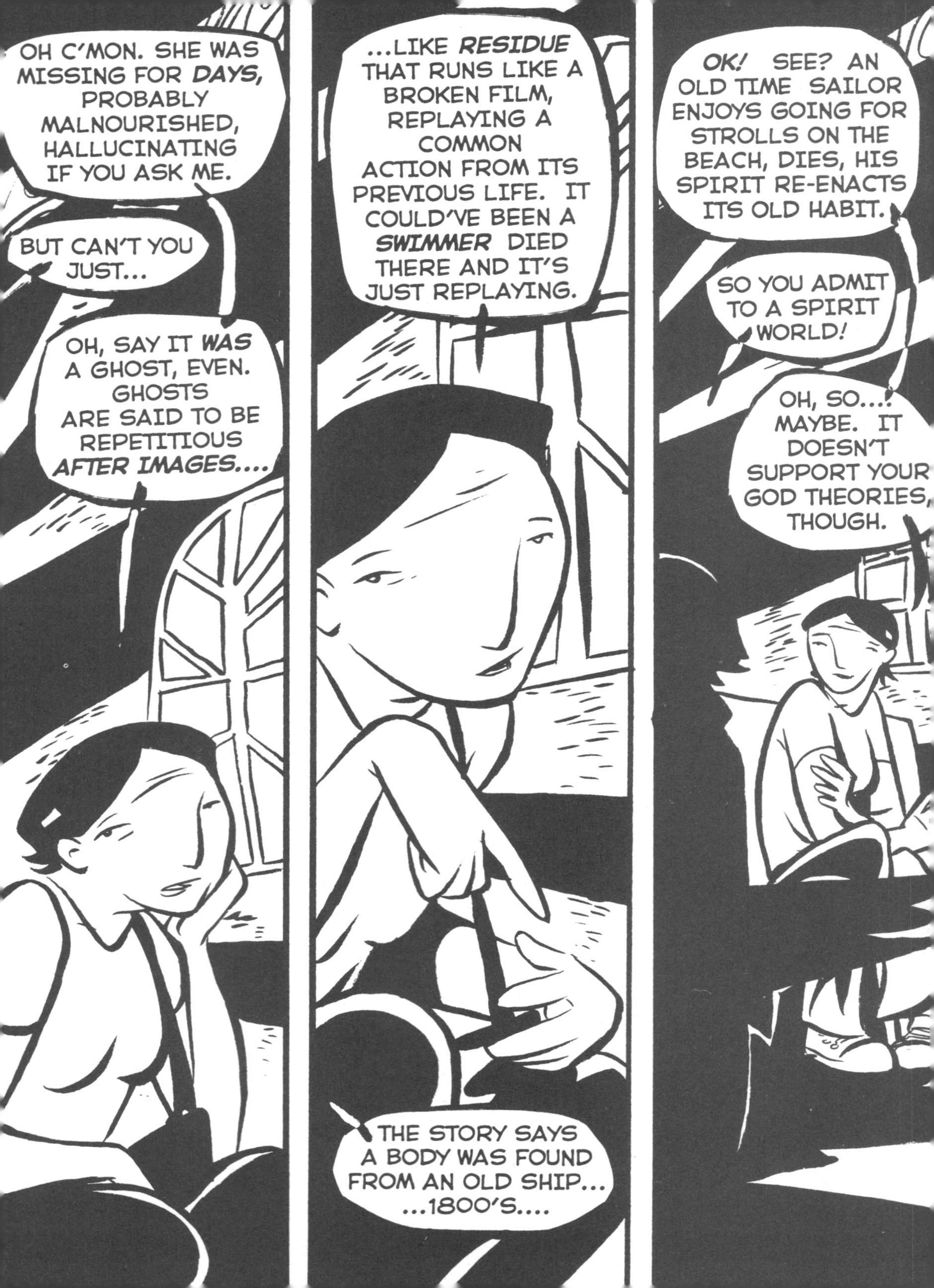
OH C'MON. SHE WAS MISSING FOR DAYS, PROBABLY MALNOURISHED, HALLUCINATING IF YOU ASK ME.
BUT CAN'T YOU JUST...
OH, SAY IT WAS A GHOST, EVEN. GHOSTS ARE SAID TO BE REPETITIOUS AFTER IMAGES....
...LIKE RESIDUE THAT RUNS LIKE A BROKEN FILM, REPLAYING A COMMON ACTION FROM ITS PREVIOUS LIFE. IT COULD'VE BEEN A SWIMMER DIED THERE AND IT'S JUST REPLAYING.
THE STORY SAYS A BODY WAS FOUND FROM AN OLD SHIP... ...1800'S....
OK! SEE? AN OLD TIME SAILOR ENJOYS GOING FOR STROLLS ON THE BEACH, DIES, HIS SPIRIT RE-ENACTS ITS OLD HABIT.
SO YOU ADMIT TO A SPIRIT WORLD!
OH, SO.... MAYBE. IT DOESN'T SUPPORT YOUR GOD THEORIES, THOUGH.

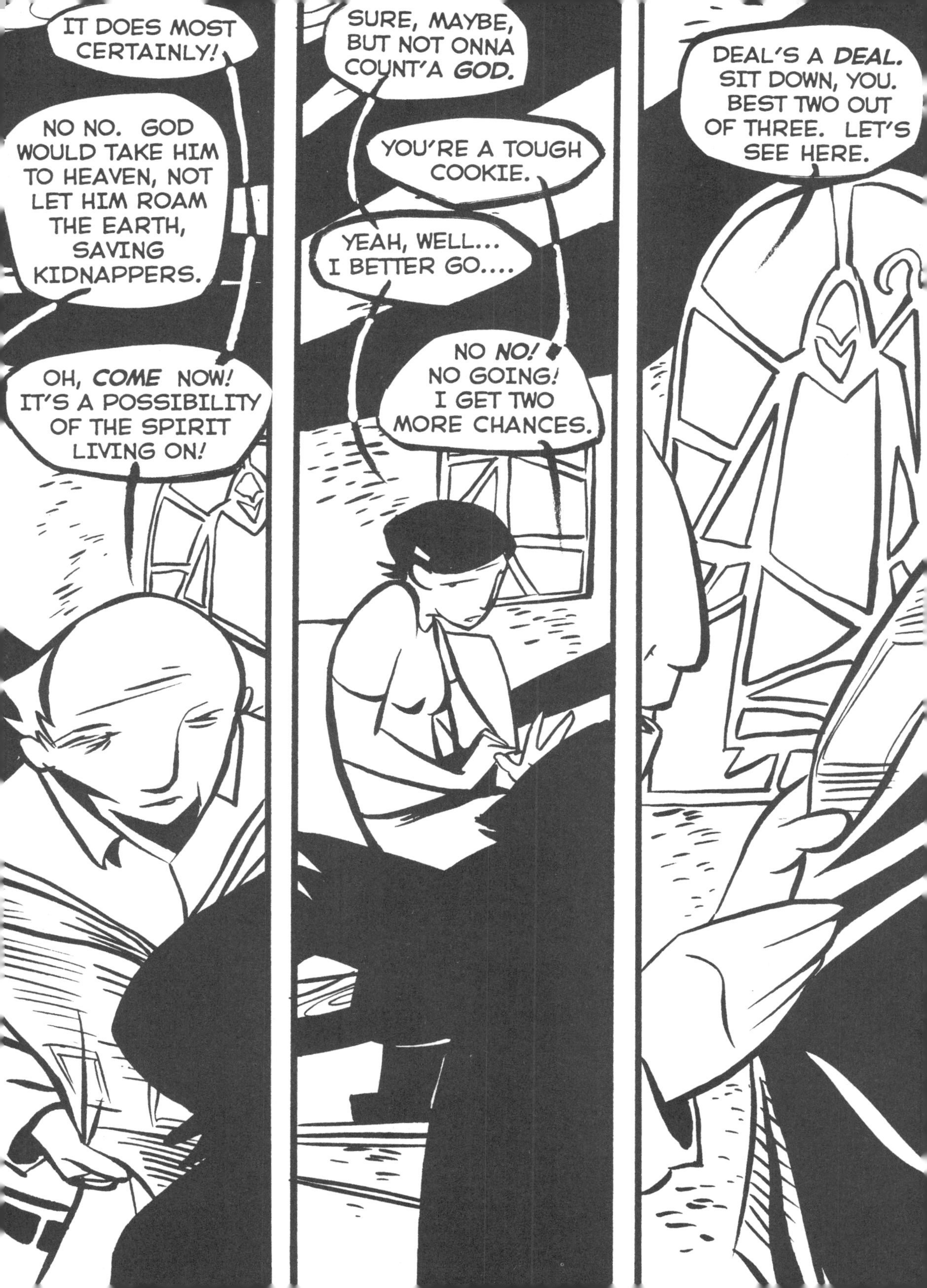

IT DOES MOST CERTAINLY!
NO NO. GOD WOULD TAKE HIM TO HEAVEN, NOT LET HIM ROAM THE EARTH, SAVING KIDNAPPERS.
OH, COME NOW! IT'S A POSSIBILITY OF THE SPIRIT LIVING ON!
SURE, MAYBE, BUT NOT ONNA COUNT'A GOD.
YOU'RE A TOUGH COOKIE.
YEAH, WELL... I BETTER GO....
NO NO! NO GOING! I GET TWO MORE CHANCES.
DEAL'S A DEAL. SIT DOWN, YOU. BEST TWO OUT OF THREE. LET'S SEE HERE.

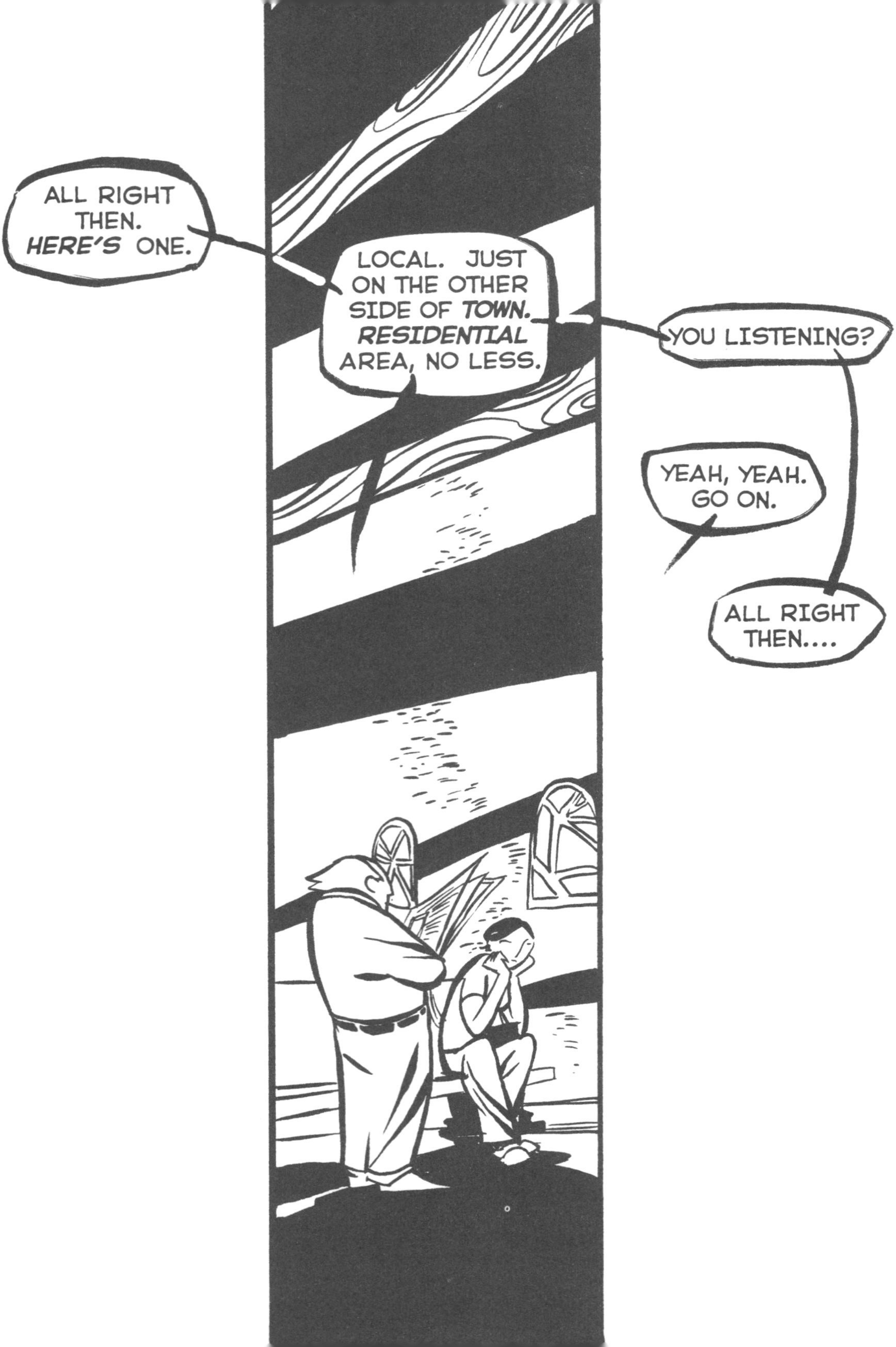
ALL RIGHT THEN. HERE'S ONE.
LOCAL. JUST ON THE OTHER SIDE OF TOWN. RESIDENTIAL AREA, NO LESS.
YOU LISTENING?
YEAH, YEAH. GO ON.
ALL RIGHT THEN....

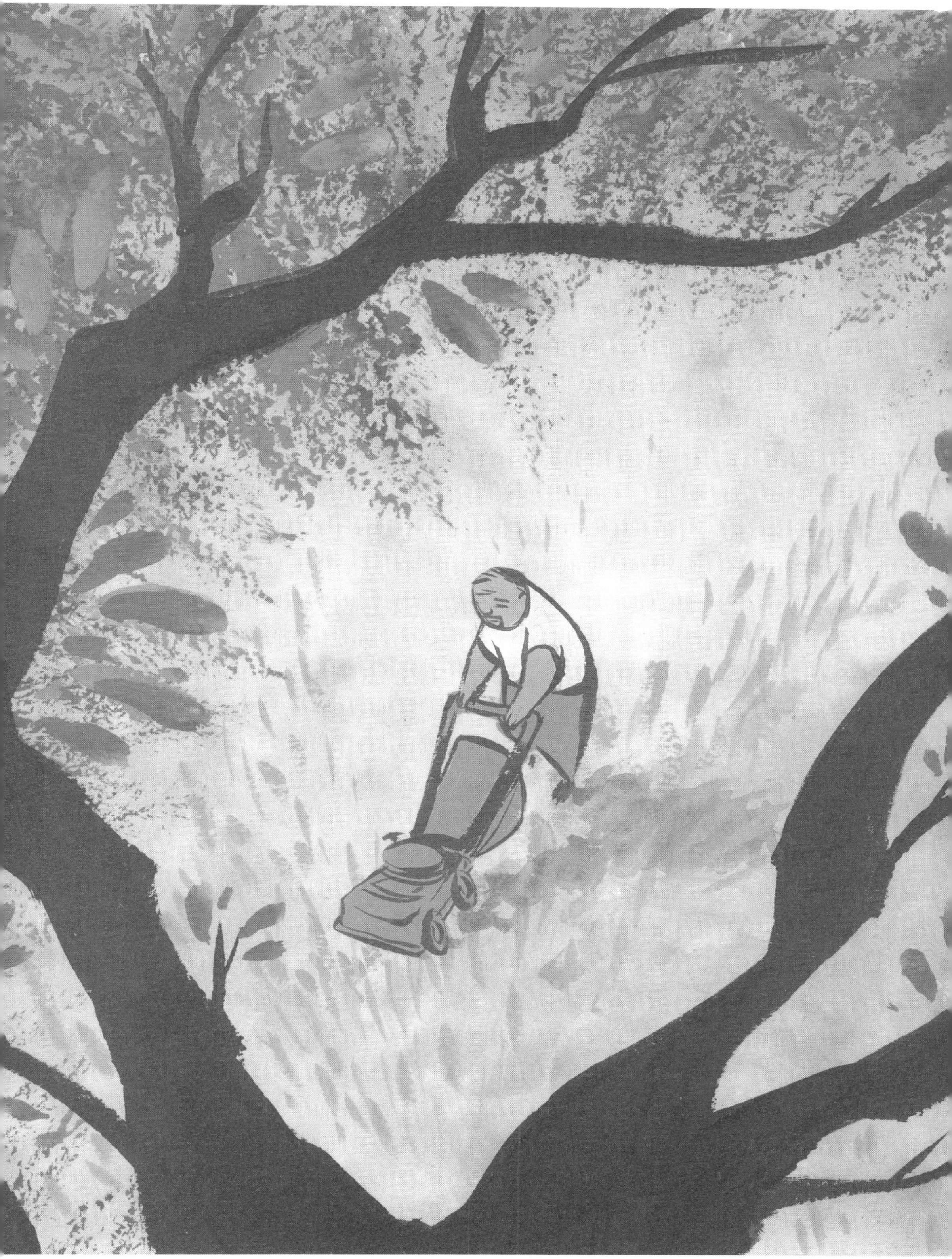

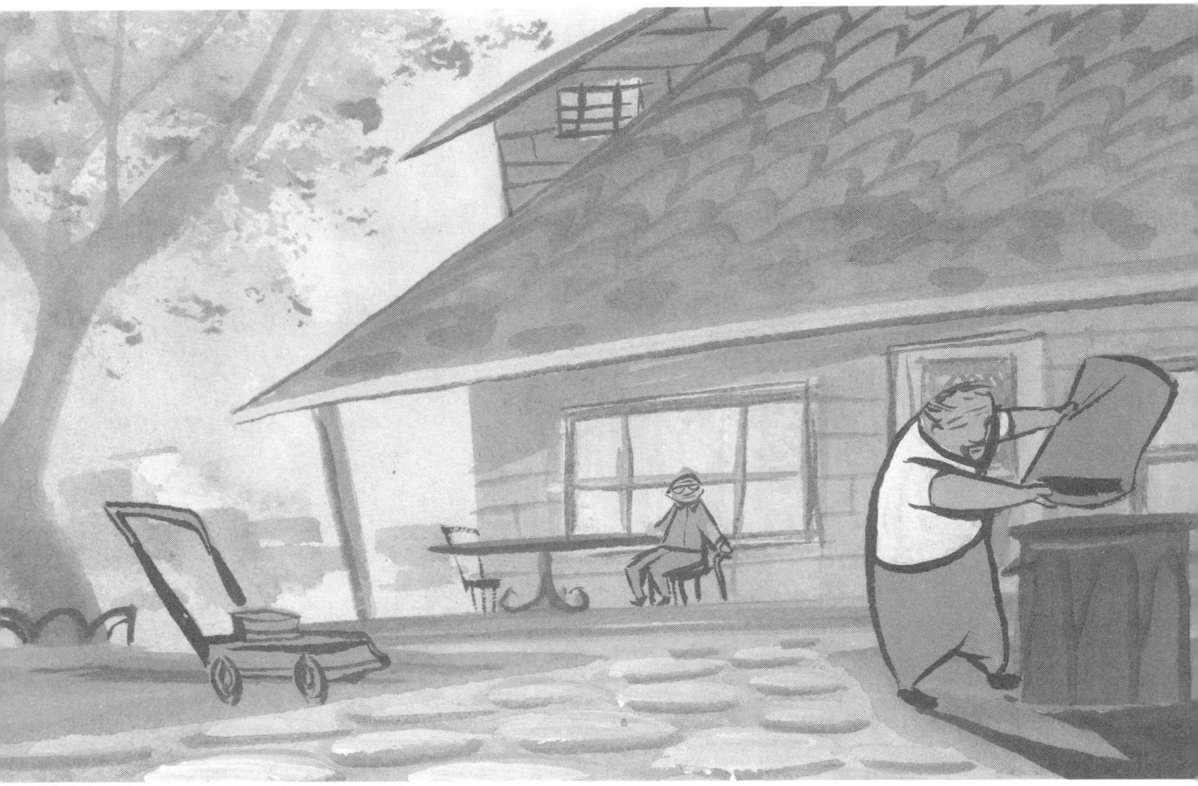

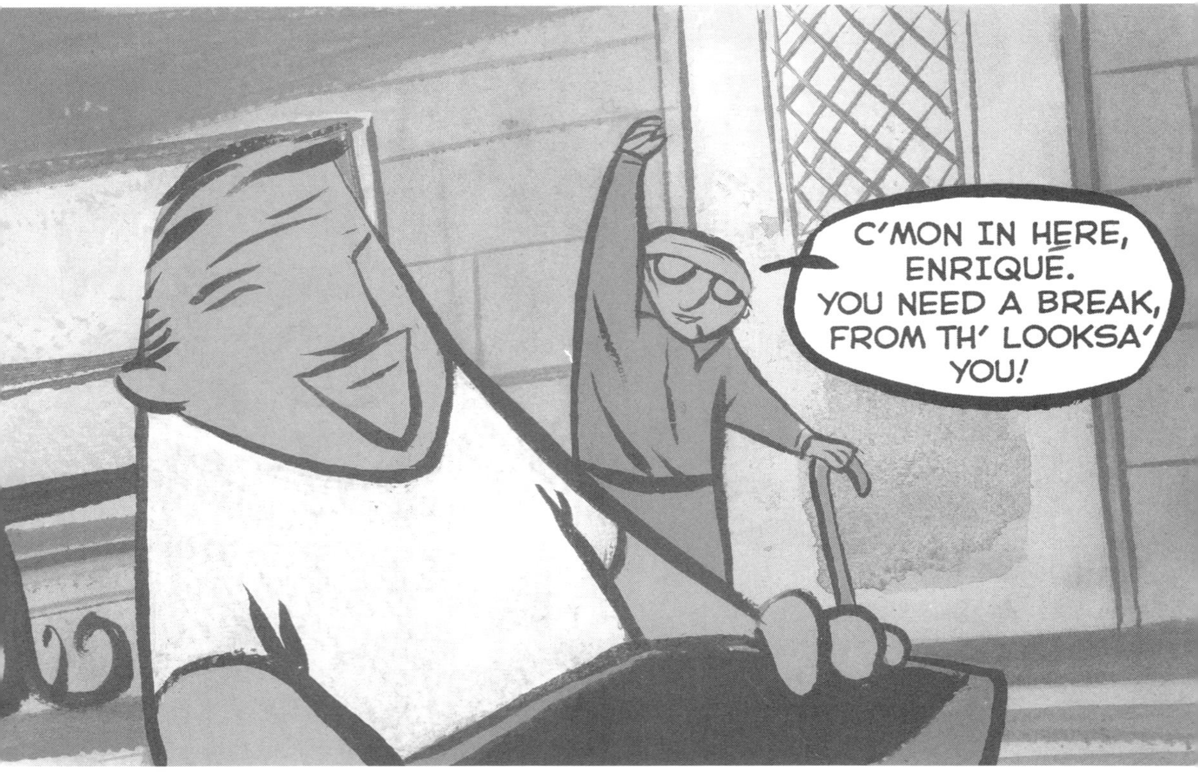
C'MON IN HERE, ENRIQUE. YOU NEED A BREAK, FROM TH' LOOKSA' YOU!

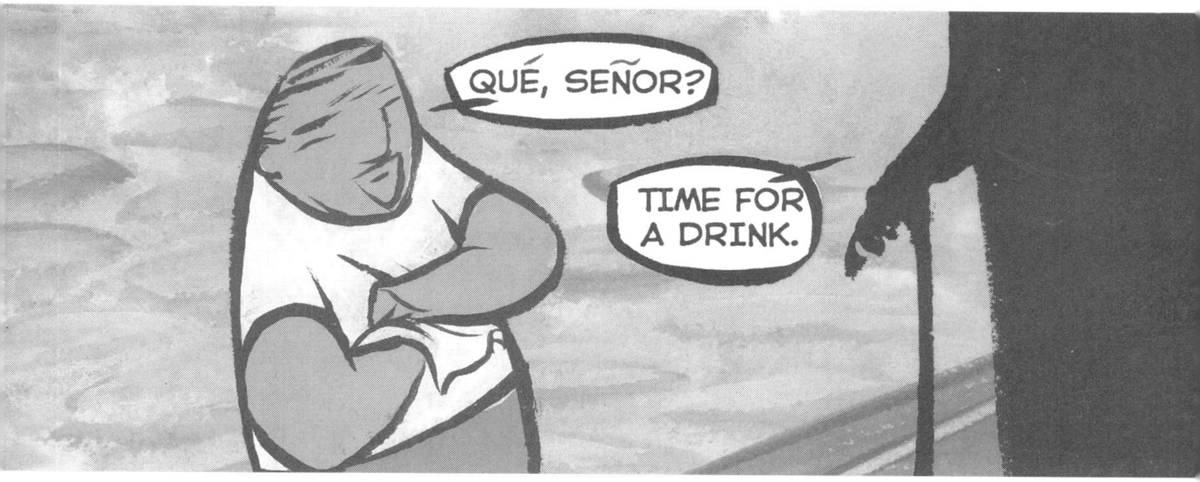
QUÉ, SEÑOR?
TIME FOR A DRINK.

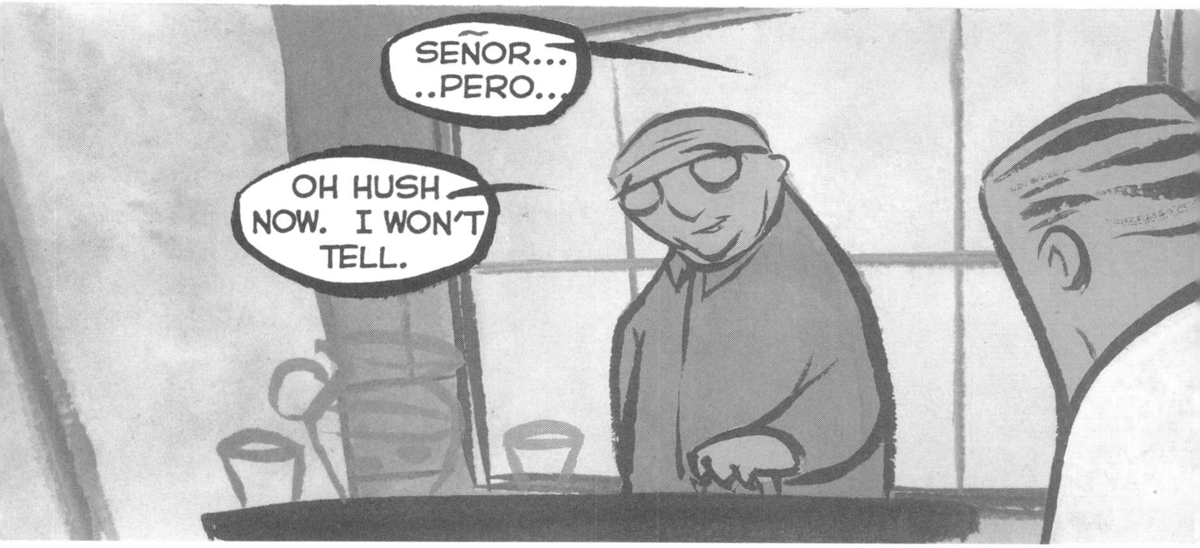
SEÑOR... ..PERO...
OH HUSH NOW. I WON'T TELL.

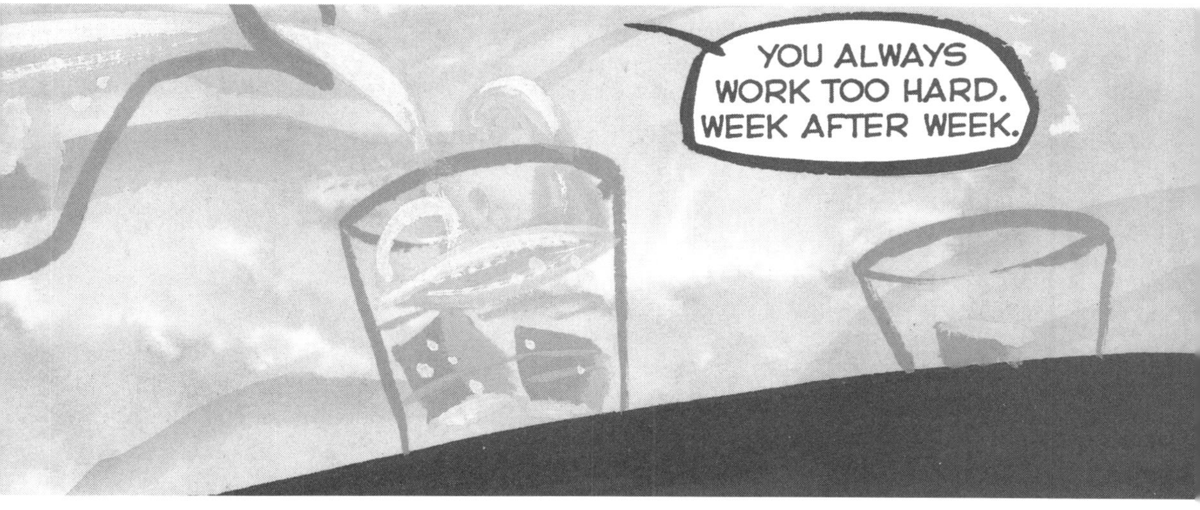
YOU ALWAYS WORK TOO HARD. WEEK AFTER WEEK.

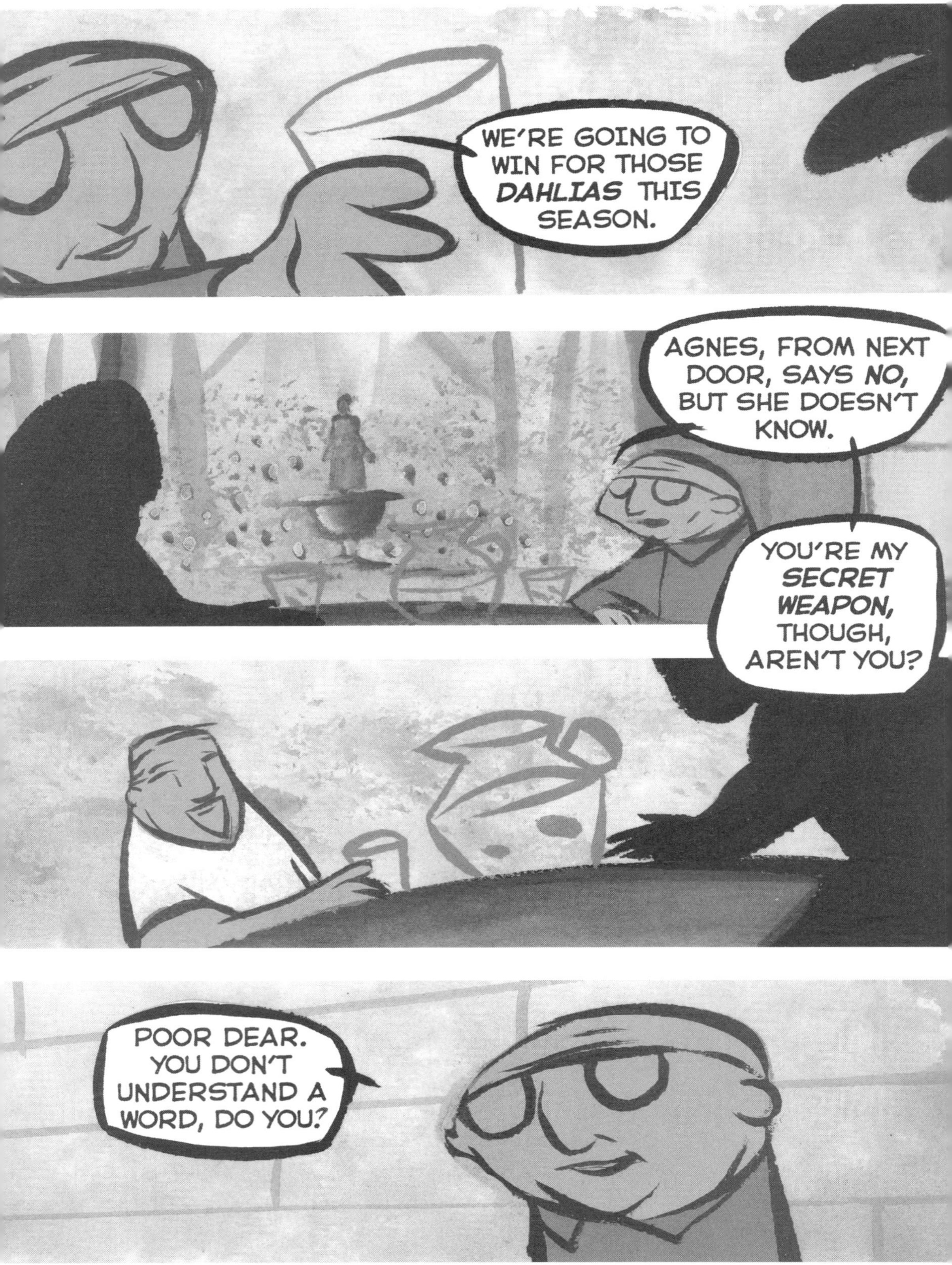
WE'RE GOING TO WIN FOR THOSE *DAHLIAS* THIS SEASON.
AGNES, FROM NEXT DOOR, SAYS *NO,* BUT SHE DOESN'T KNOW.
YOU'RE MY *SECRET WEAPON,* THOUGH, AREN'T YOU?
POOR DEAR. YOU DON'T UNDERSTAND A WORD, DO YOU?

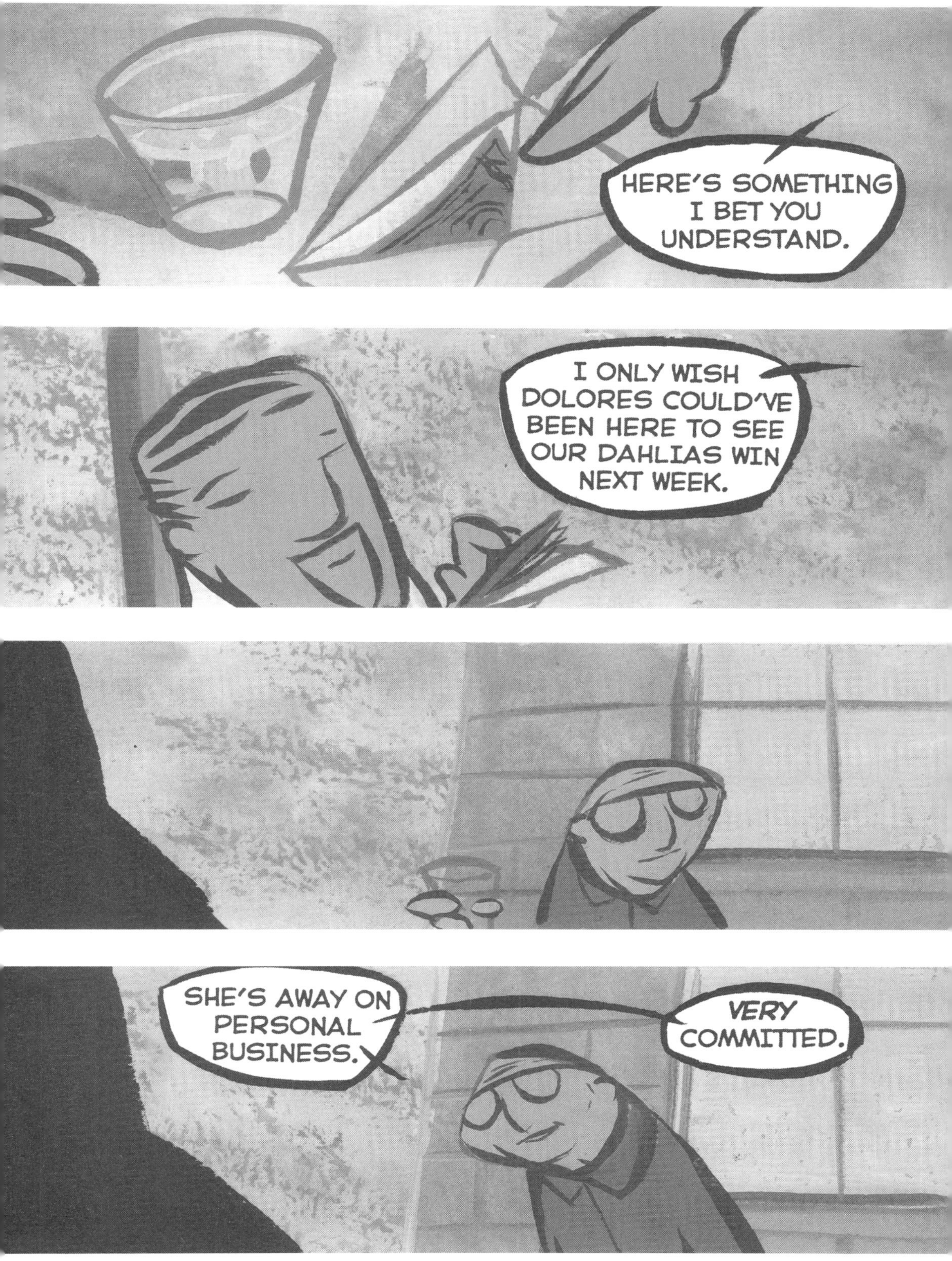
HERE'S SOMETHING I BET YOU UNDERSTAND.
I ONLY WISH DOLORES COULD'VE BEEN HERE TO SEE OUR DAHLIAS WIN NEXT WEEK.
SHE'S AWAY ON PERSONAL BUSINESS.
VERY COMMITTED.

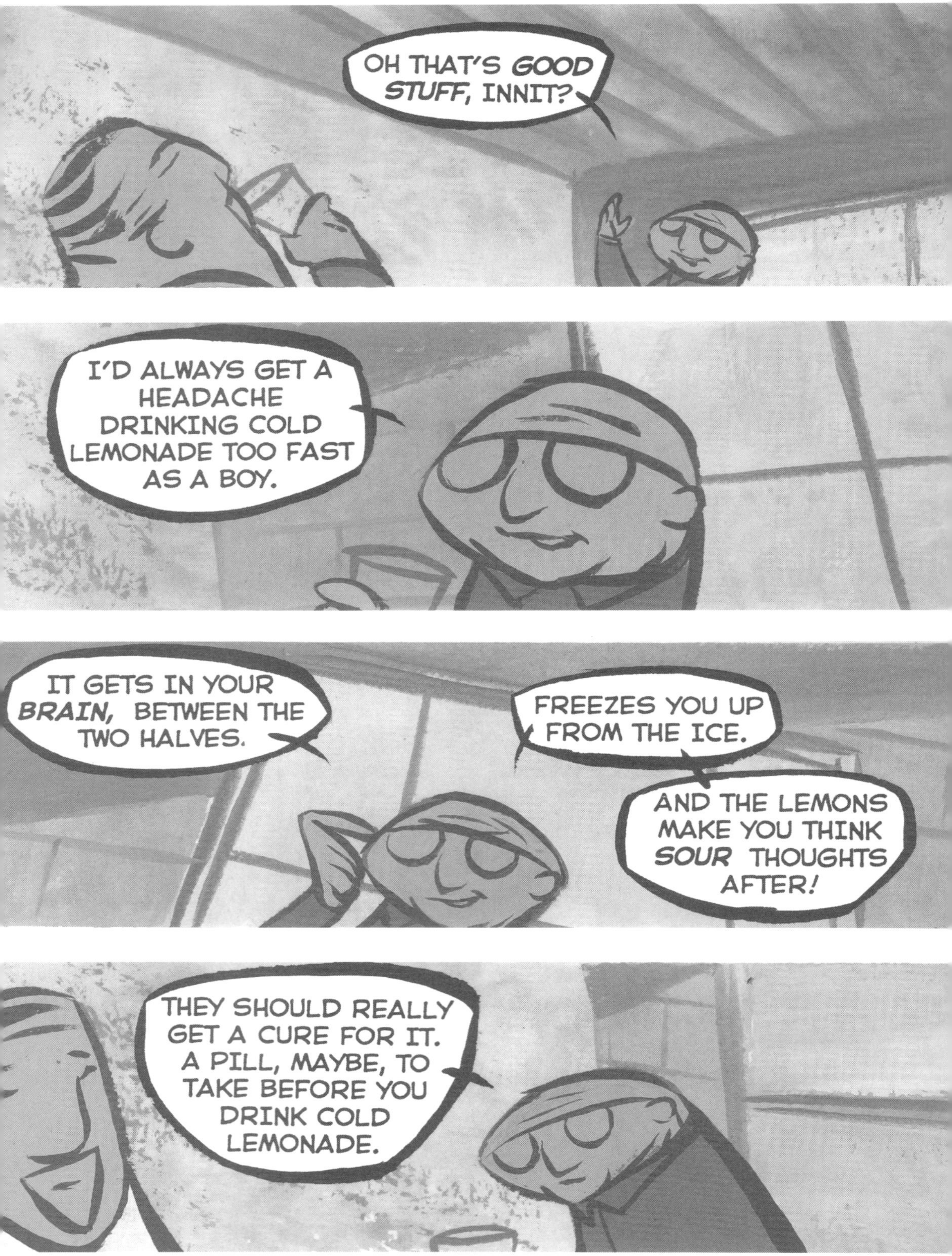
OH THAT'S *GOOD STUFF*, INNIT?
I'D ALWAYS GET A HEADACHE DRINKING COLD LEMONADE TOO FAST AS A BOY.
IT GETS IN YOUR *BRAIN*, BETWEEN THE TWO HALVES.
FREEZES YOU UP FROM THE ICE.
AND THE LEMONS MAKE YOU THINK *SOUR* THOUGHTS AFTER!
THEY SHOULD REALLY GET A CURE FOR IT. A PILL, MAYBE, TO TAKE BEFORE YOU DRINK COLD LEMONADE.

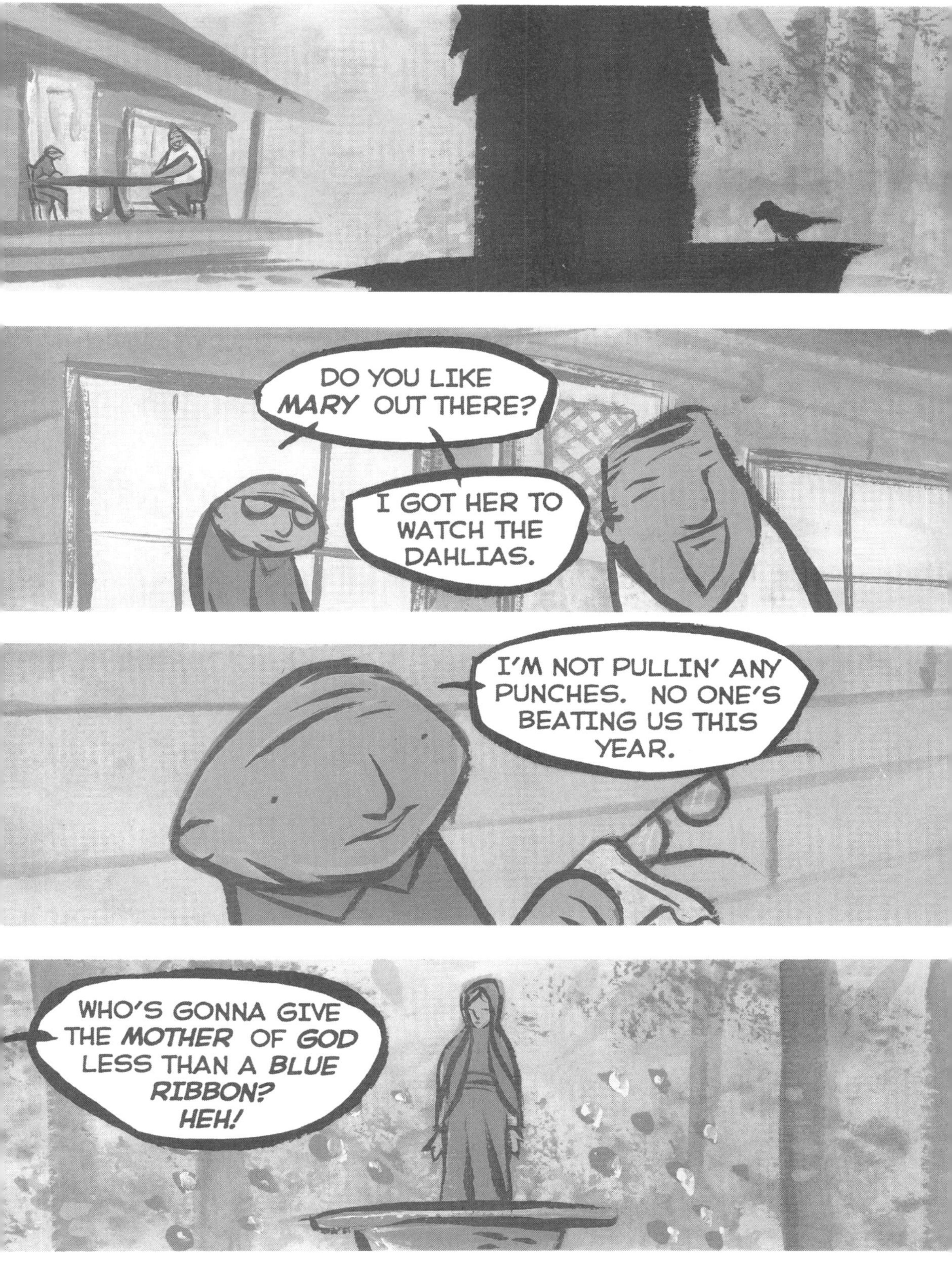
DO YOU LIKE MARY OUT THERE?
I GOT HER TO WATCH THE DAHLIAS.
I'M NOT PULLIN' ANY PUNCHES. NO ONE'S BEATING US THIS YEAR.
WHO'S GONNA GIVE THE MOTHER OF GOD LESS THAN A BLUE RIBBON? HEH!

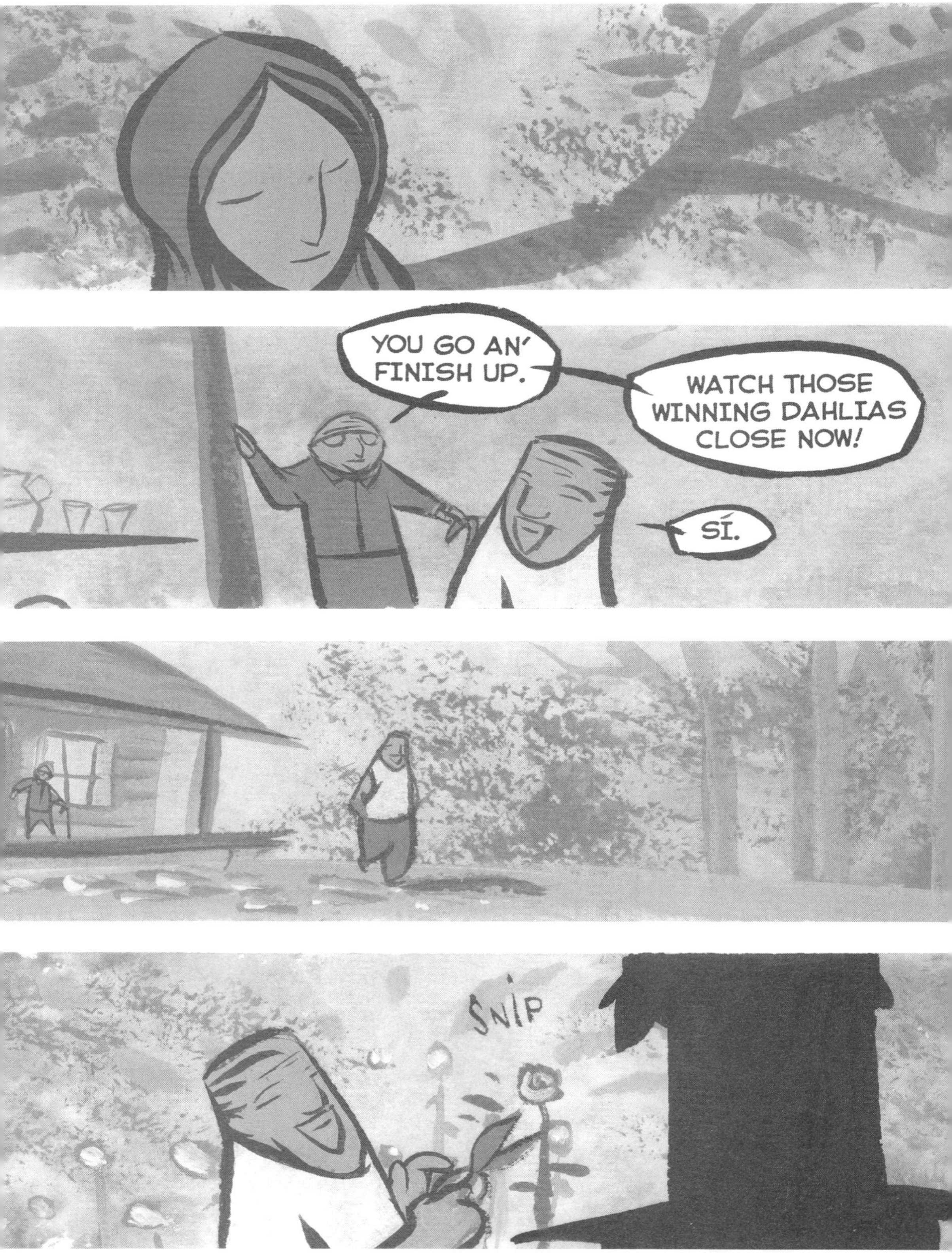
YOU GO AN' FINISH UP.
WATCH THOSE WINNING DAHLIAS CLOSE NOW!
SÍ.
SNIP

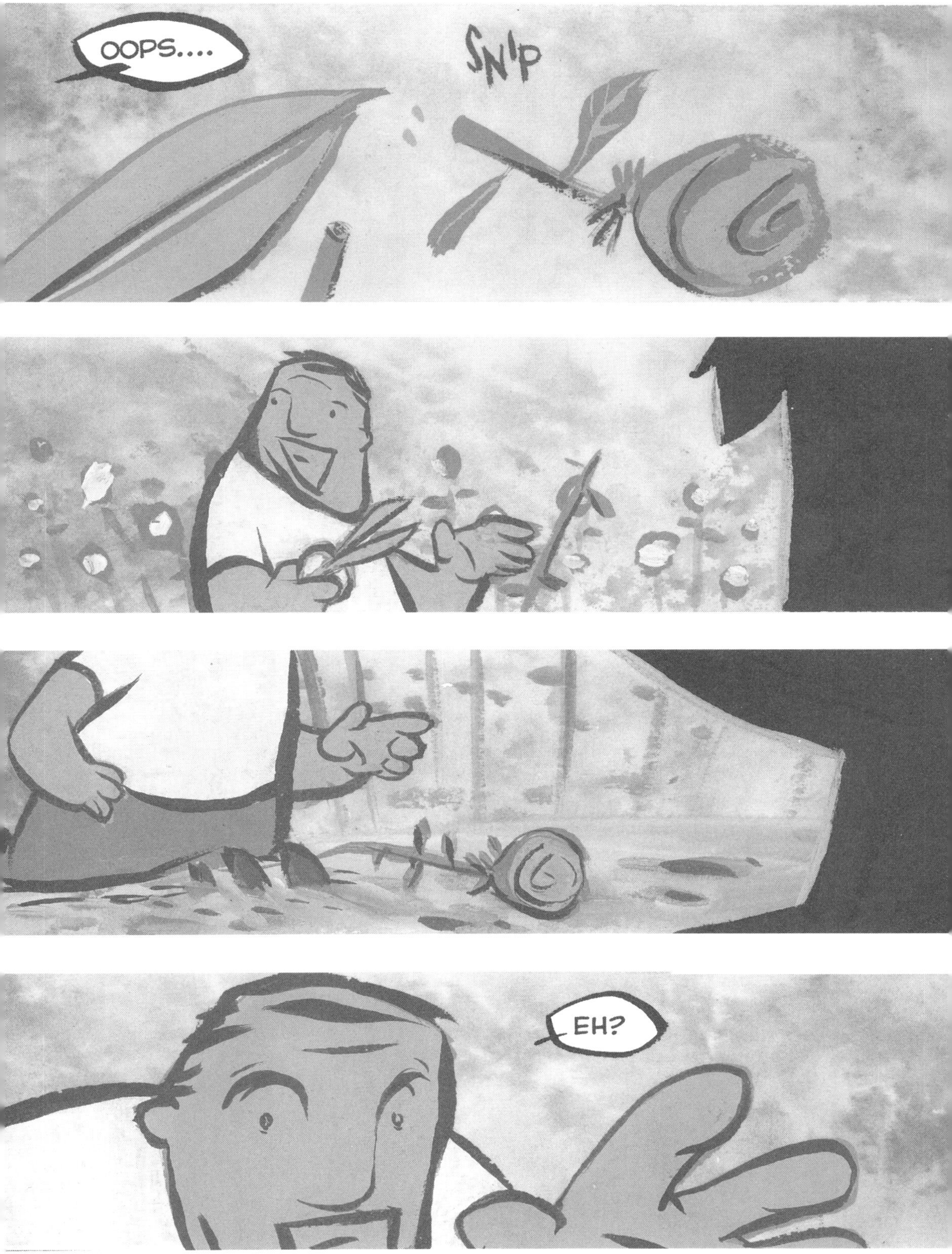
OOPS....
SNIP
EH?

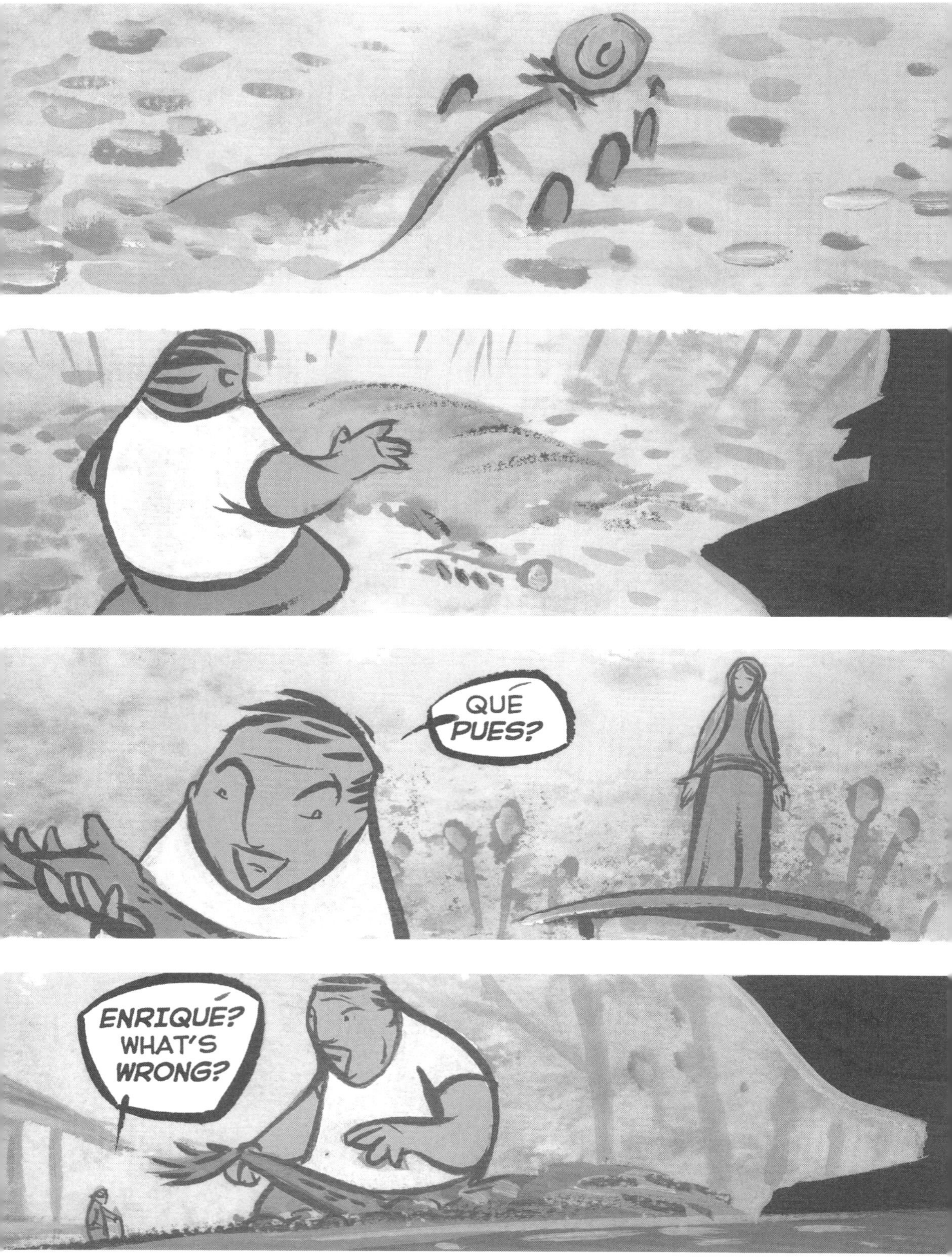
QUÉ PUES?
ENRIQUE? WHAT'S WRONG?

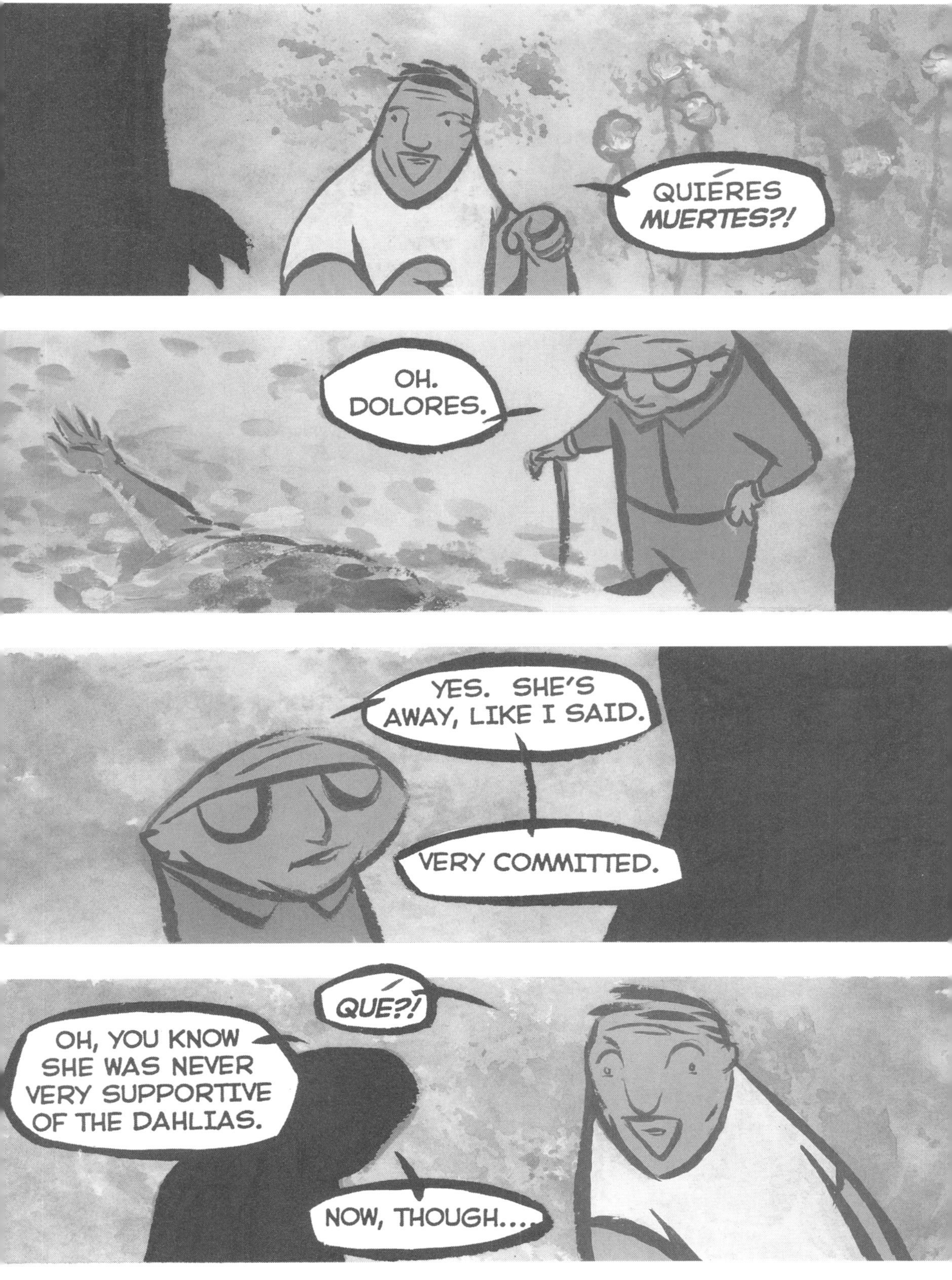

QUIÉRES MUERTES?!
OH. DOLORES.
YES. SHE'S AWAY, LIKE I SAID.
VERY COMMITTED.
QUÉ?!
OH, YOU KNOW SHE WAS NEVER VERY SUPPORTIVE OF THE DAHLIAS.
NOW, THOUGH...

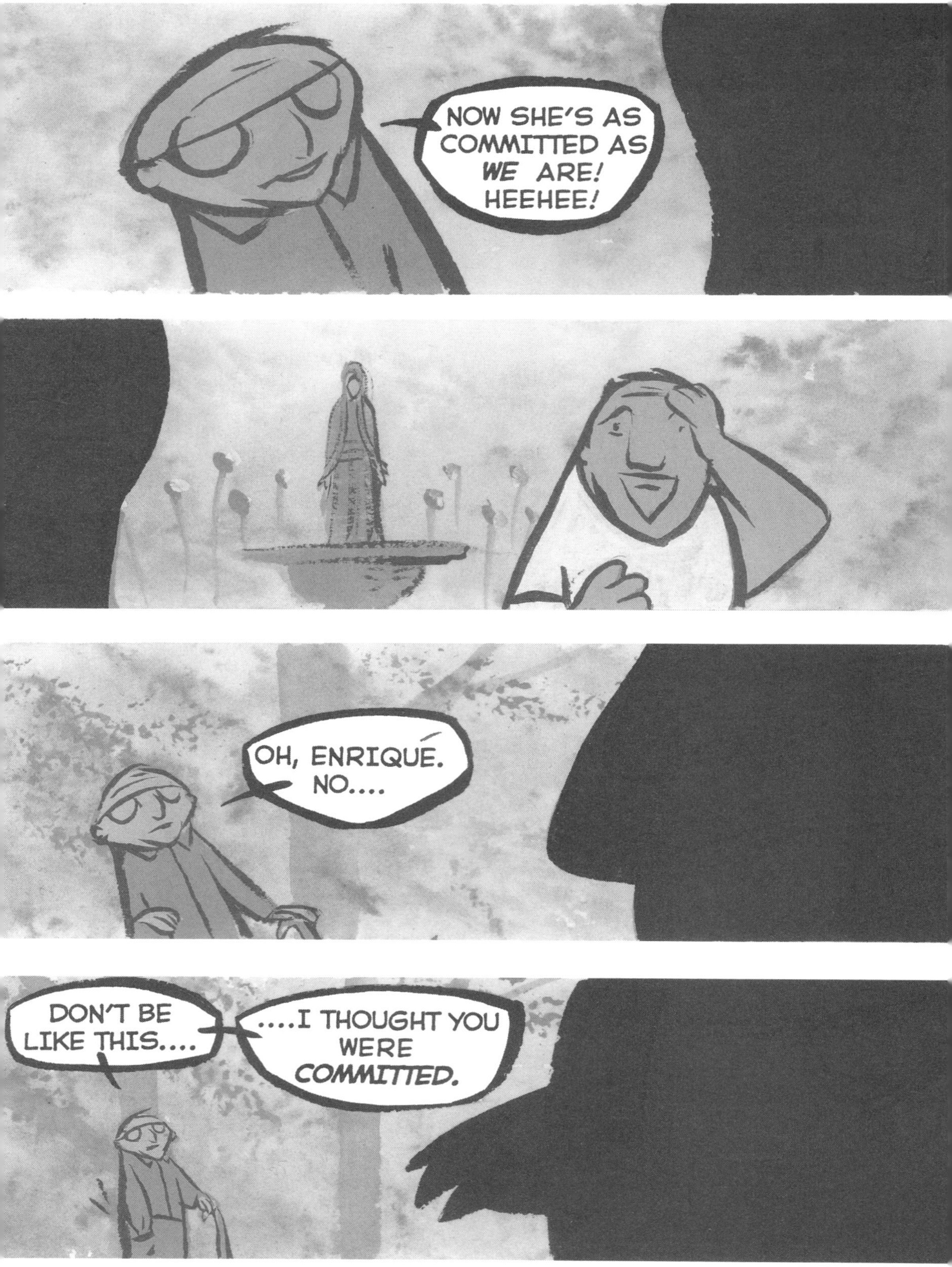
NOW SHE'S AS COMMITTED AS *WE* ARE! HEEHEE!
OH, ENRIQUÉ. NO....
DON'T BE LIKE THIS....
....I THOUGHT YOU WERE *COMMITTED.*

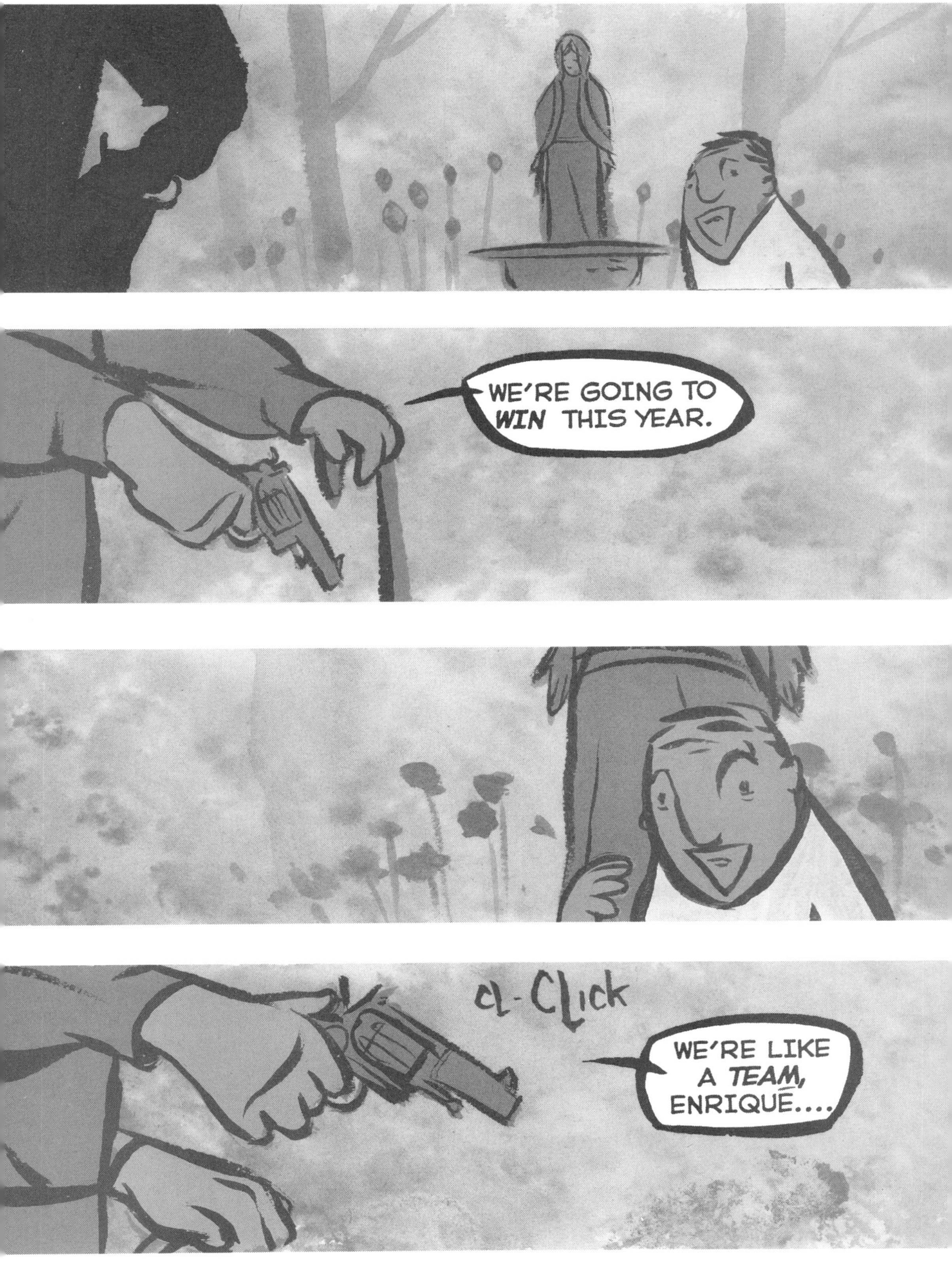
WE'RE GOING TO WIN THIS YEAR.
CL-CLICK
WE'RE LIKE A TEAM, ENRIQUE....

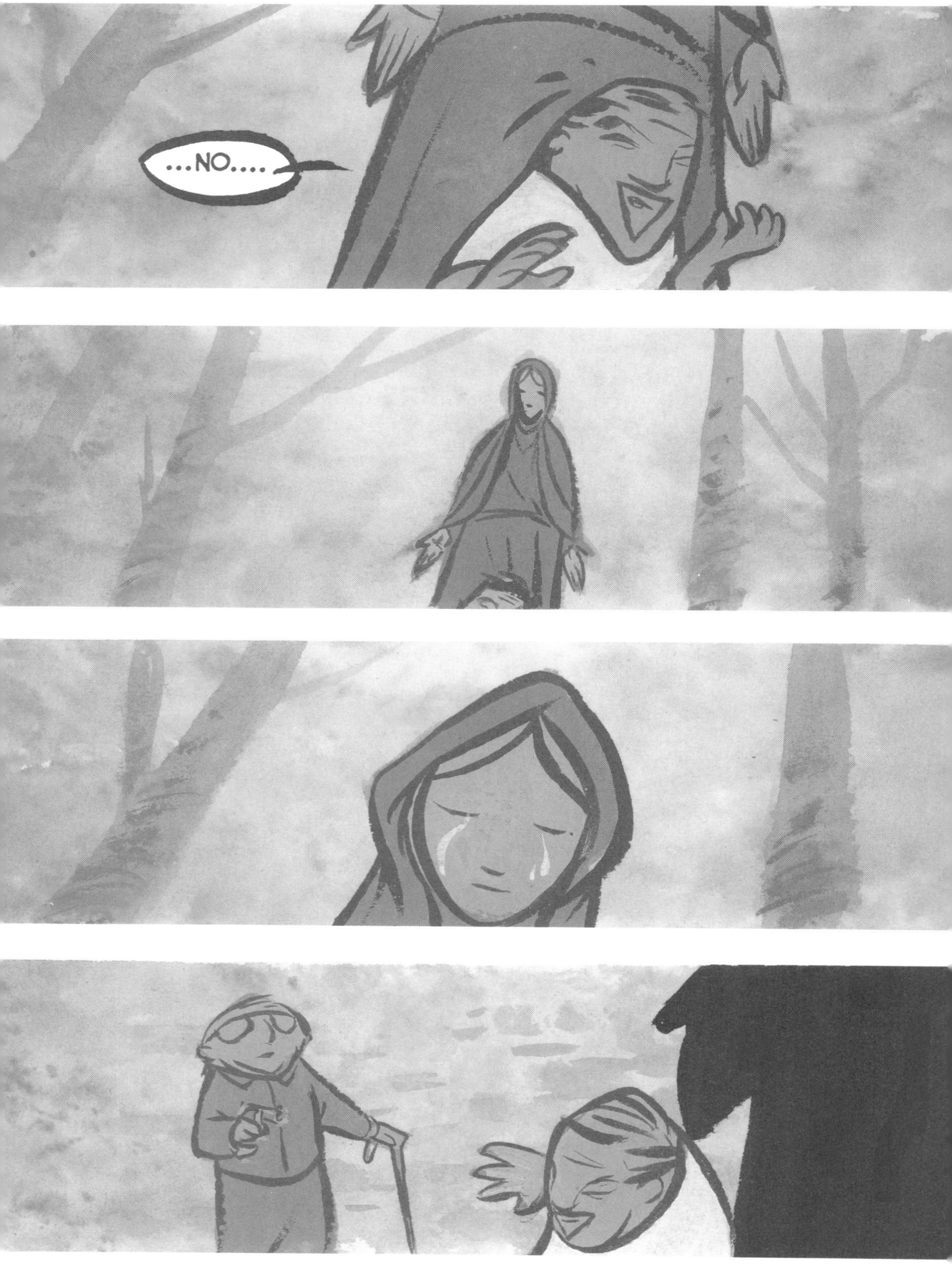
...NO....

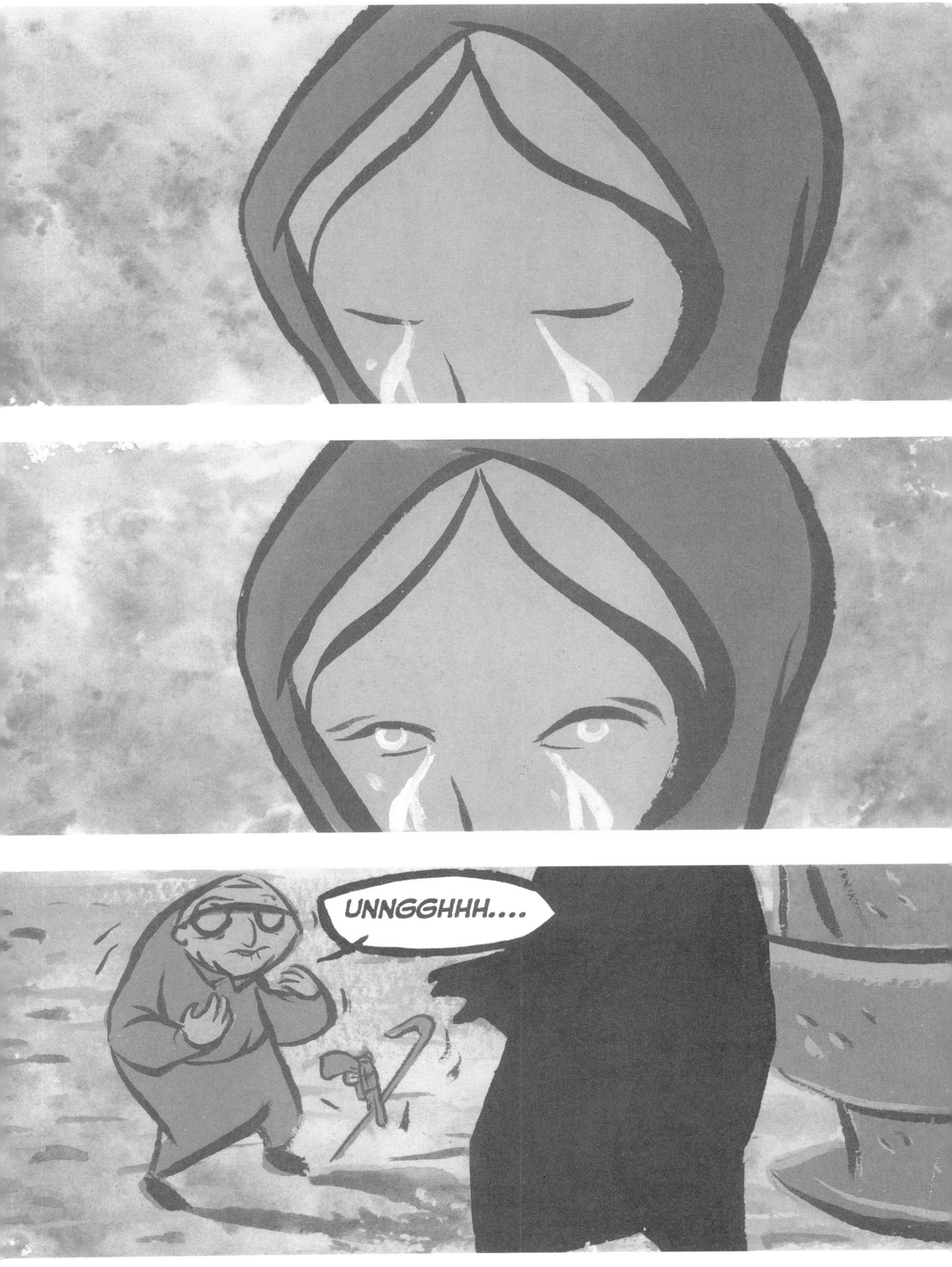
UNNGGHHH....

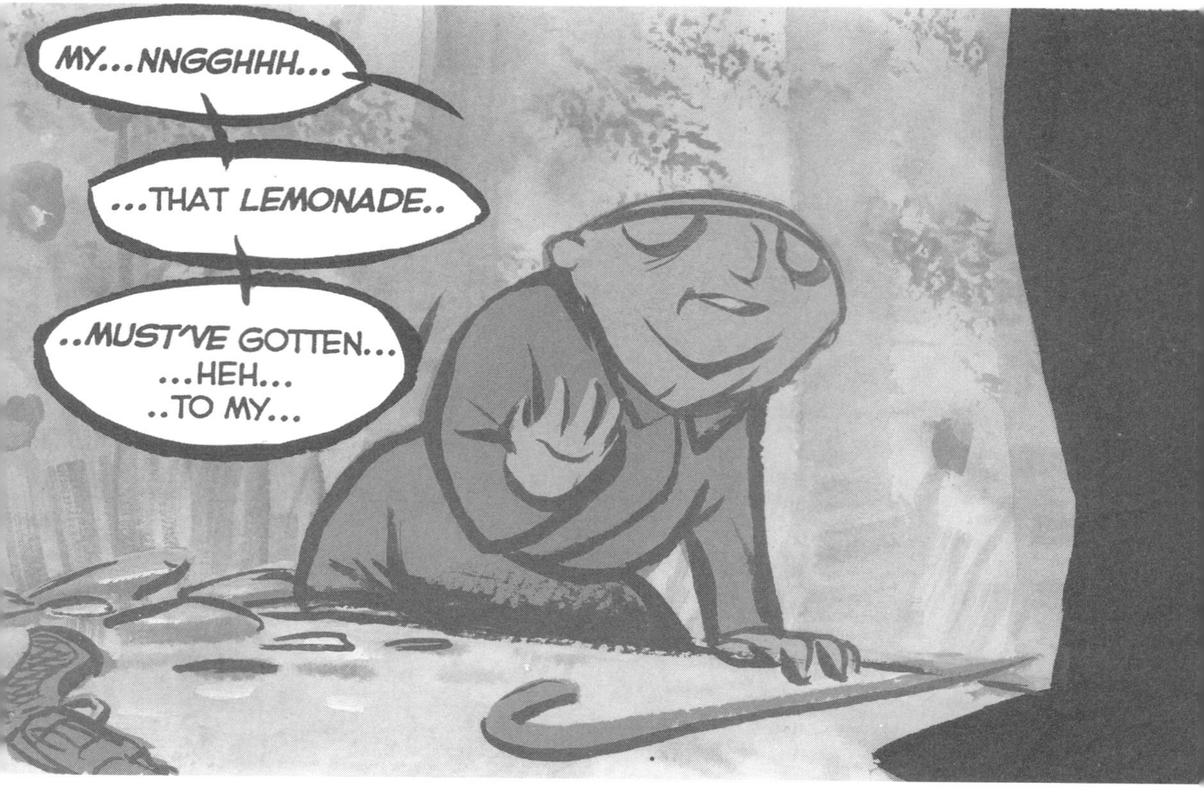
MY...NNGGHHH...
...THAT LEMONADE..
..MUST'VE GOTTEN... ...HEH... ..TO MY...

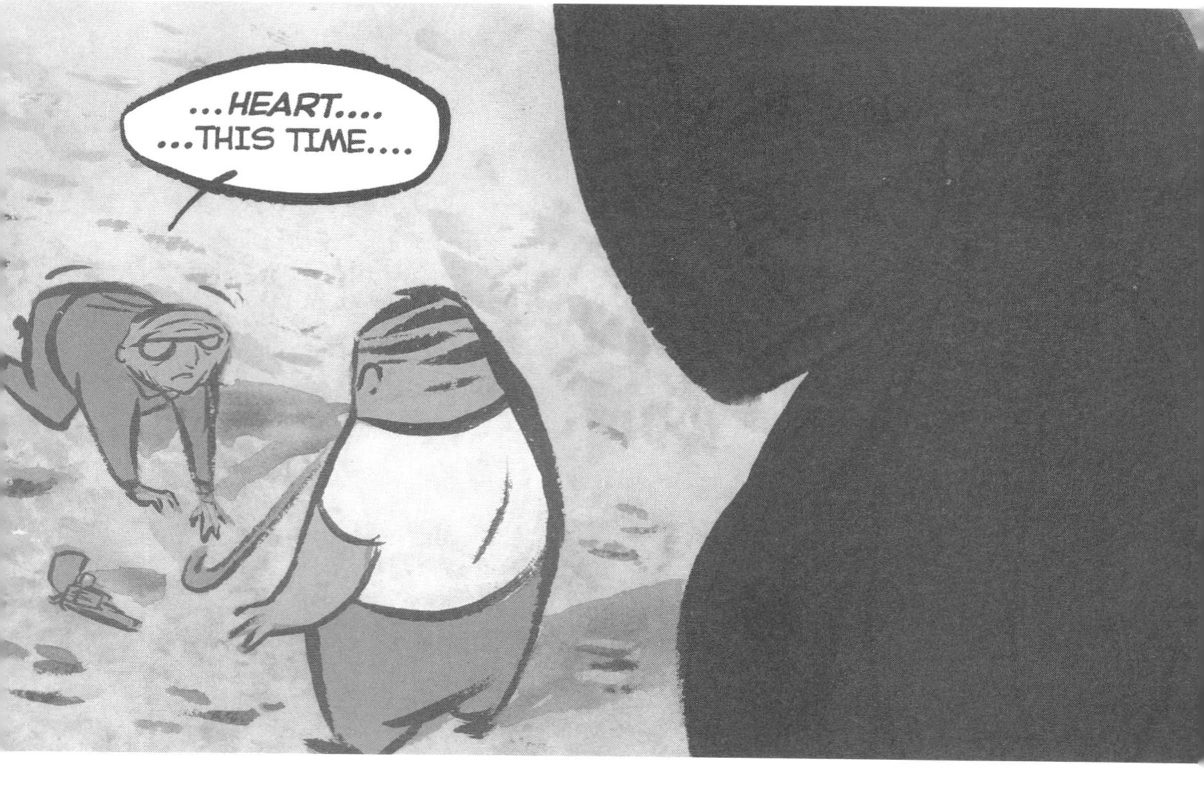
...HEART.... ...THIS TIME....

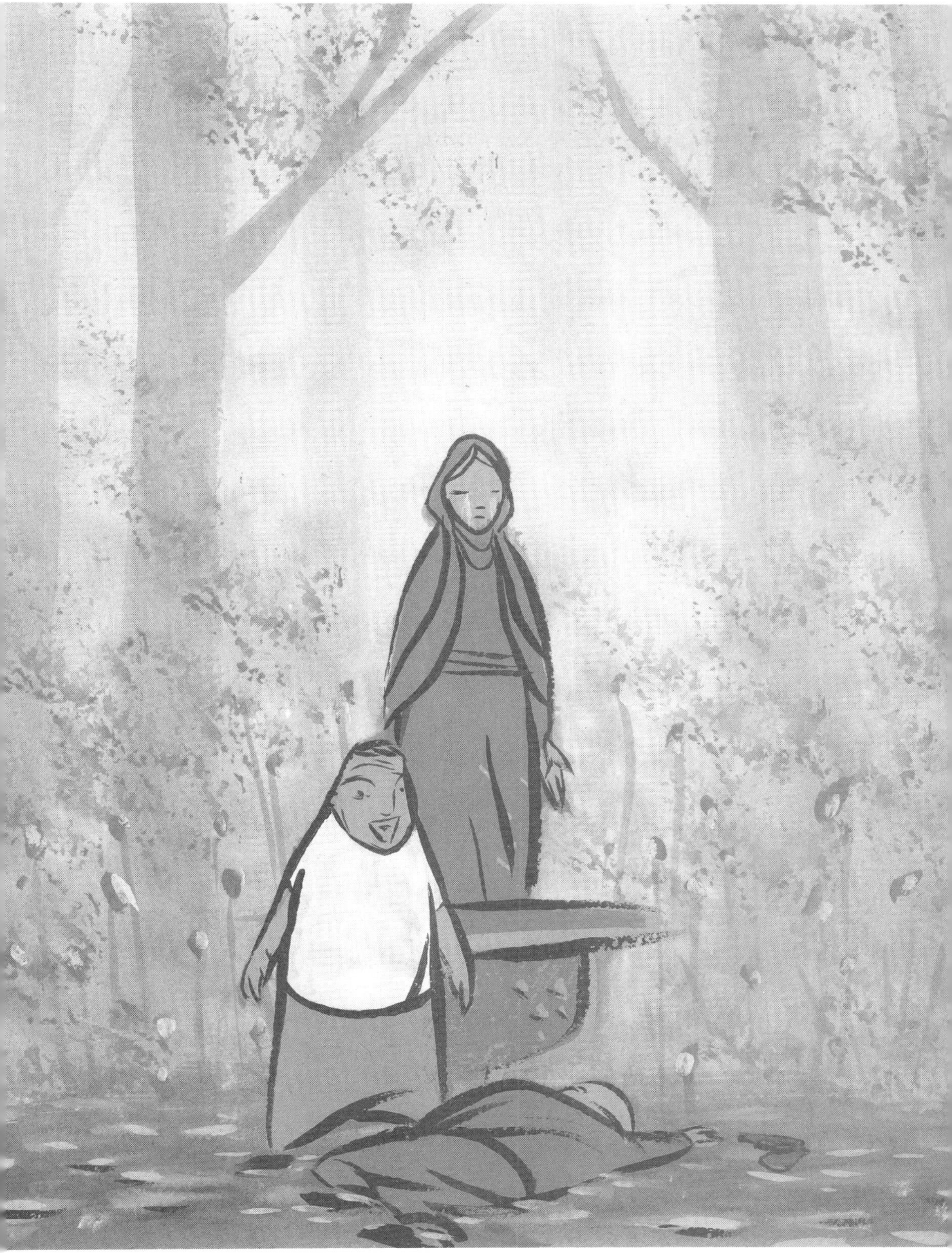

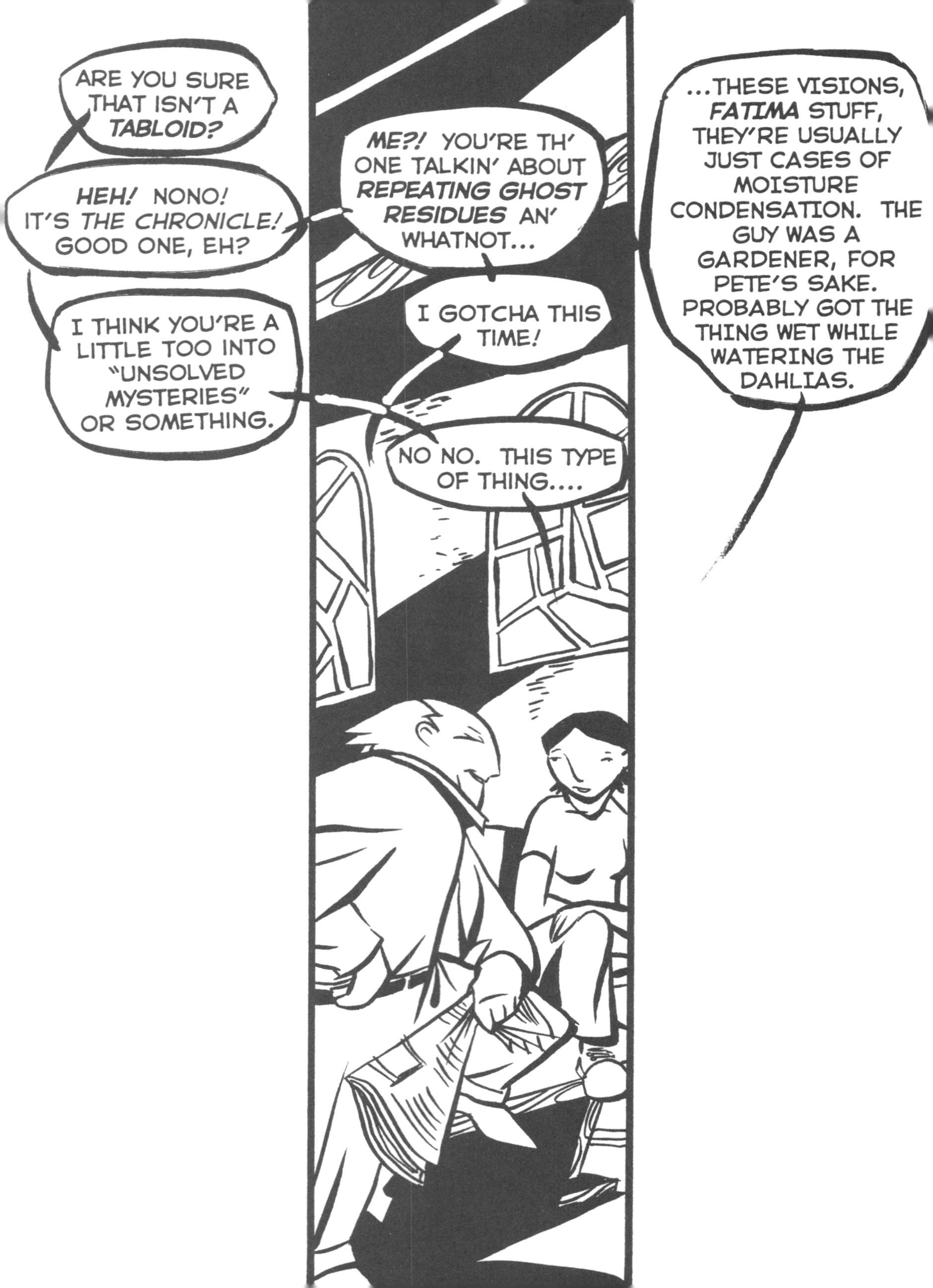
ARE YOU SURE THAT ISN'T A *TABLOID?*
HEH! NONO! IT'S *THE CHRONICLE!* GOOD ONE, EH?
I THINK YOU'RE A LITTLE TOO INTO "UNSOLVED MYSTERIES" OR SOMETHING.
ME?! YOU'RE TH' ONE TALKIN' ABOUT *REPEATING GHOST RESIDUES* AN' WHATNOT...
I GOTCHA THIS TIME!
NO NO. THIS TYPE OF THING....
...THESE VISIONS, *FATIMA* STUFF, THEY'RE USUALLY JUST CASES OF MOISTURE CONDENSATION. THE GUY WAS A GARDENER, FOR PETE'S SAKE. PROBABLY GOT THE THING WET WHILE WATERING THE DAHLIAS.

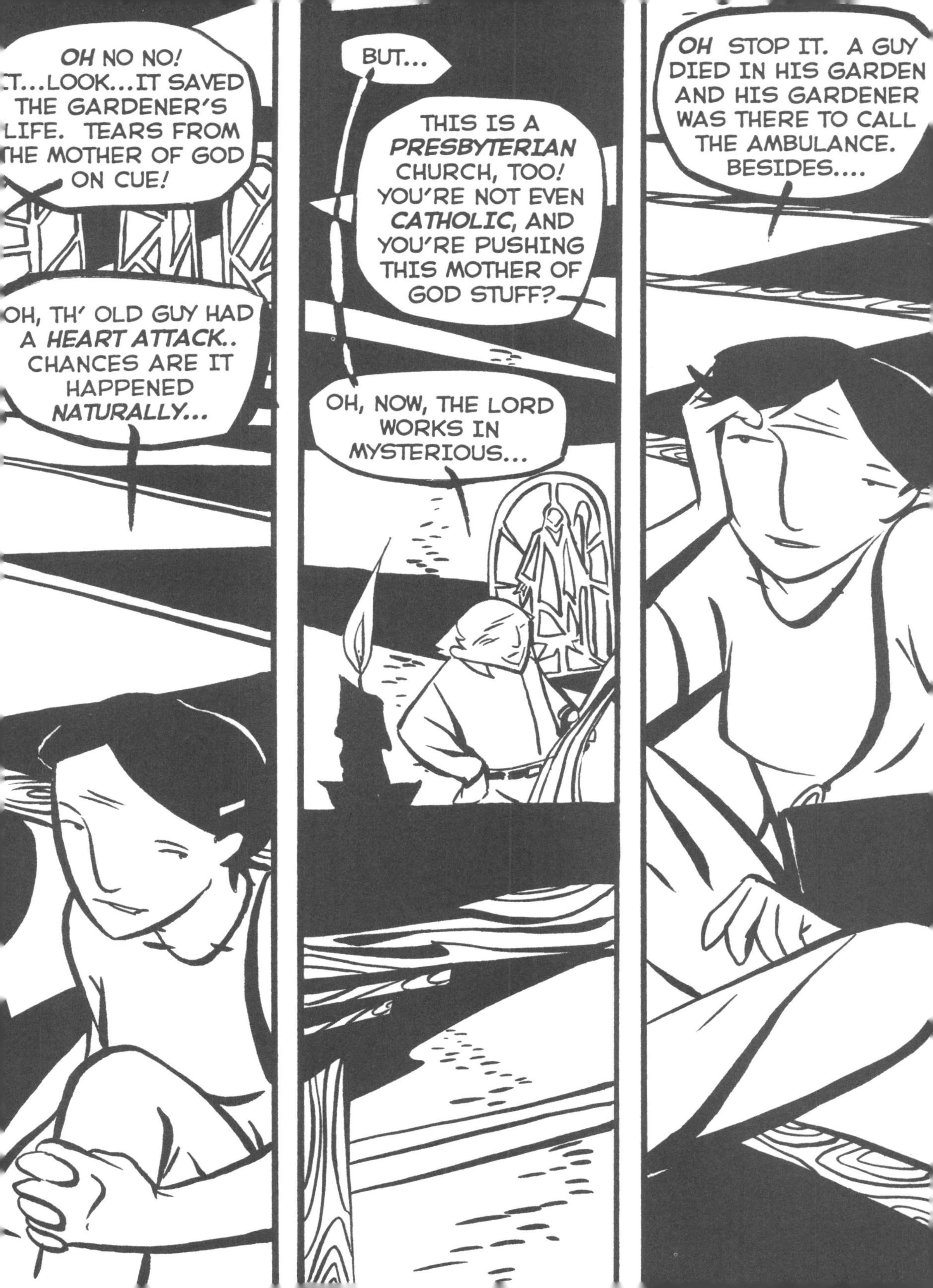
OH NO NO! IT...LOOK...IT SAVED THE GARDENER'S LIFE. TEARS FROM THE MOTHER OF GOD ON CUE!
OH, TH' OLD GUY HAD A HEART ATTACK.. CHANCES ARE IT HAPPENED NATURALLY...
BUT...
THIS IS A PRESBYTERIAN CHURCH, TOO! YOU'RE NOT EVEN CATHOLIC, AND YOU'RE PUSHING THIS MOTHER OF GOD STUFF?
OH, NOW, THE LORD WORKS IN MYSTERIOUS...
OH STOP IT. A GUY DIED IN HIS GARDEN AND HIS GARDENER WAS THERE TO CALL THE AMBULANCE. BESIDES....

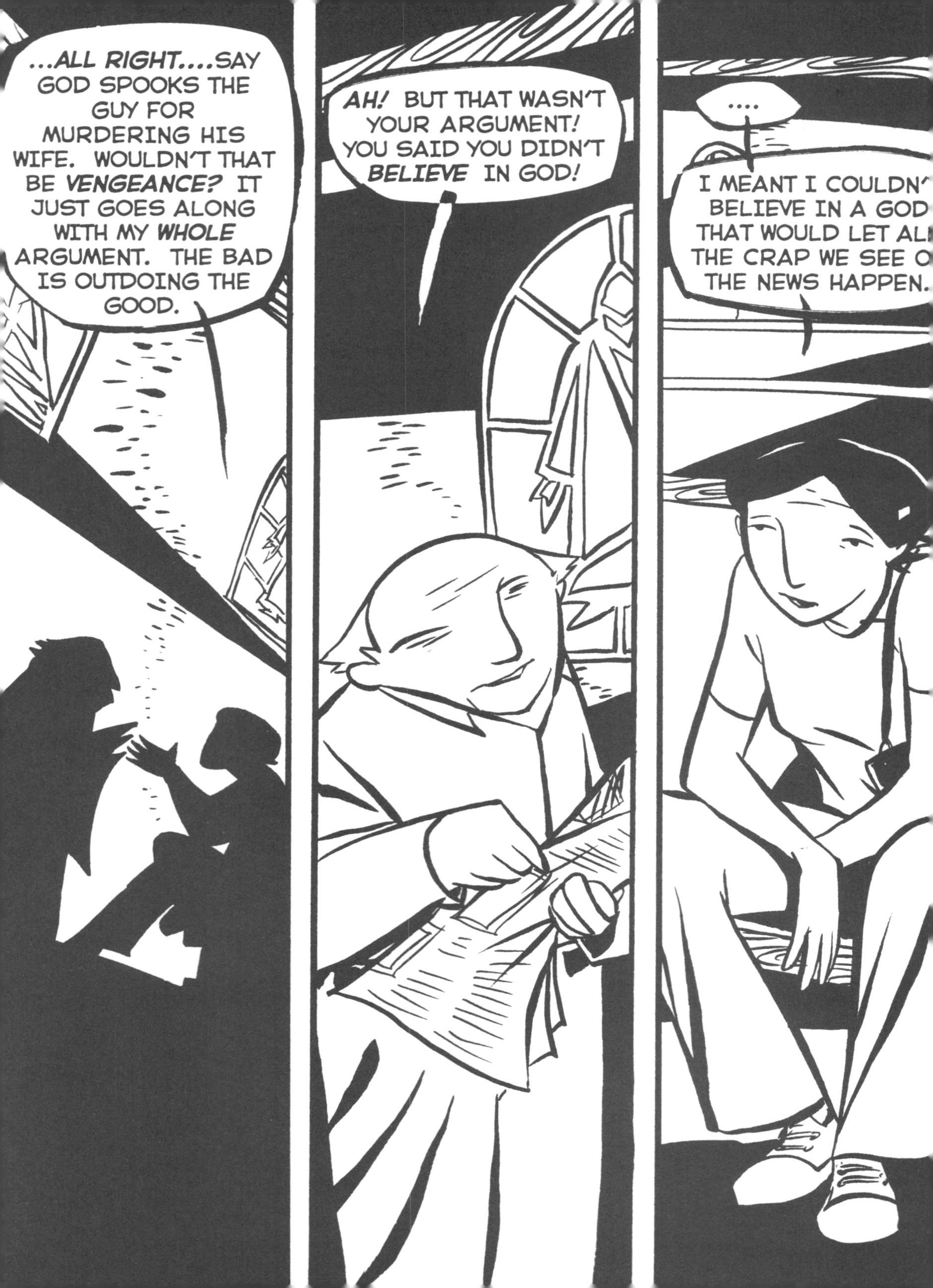
...ALL RIGHT....SAY GOD SPOOKS THE GUY FOR MURDERING HIS WIFE. WOULDN'T THAT BE VENGEANCE? IT JUST GOES ALONG WITH MY WHOLE ARGUMENT. THE BAD IS OUTDOING THE GOOD.
AH! BUT THAT WASN'T YOUR ARGUMENT! YOU SAID YOU DIDN'T BELIEVE IN GOD!
....
I MEANT I COULDN'T BELIEVE IN A GOD THAT WOULD LET ALL THE CRAP WE SEE ON THE NEWS HAPPEN.

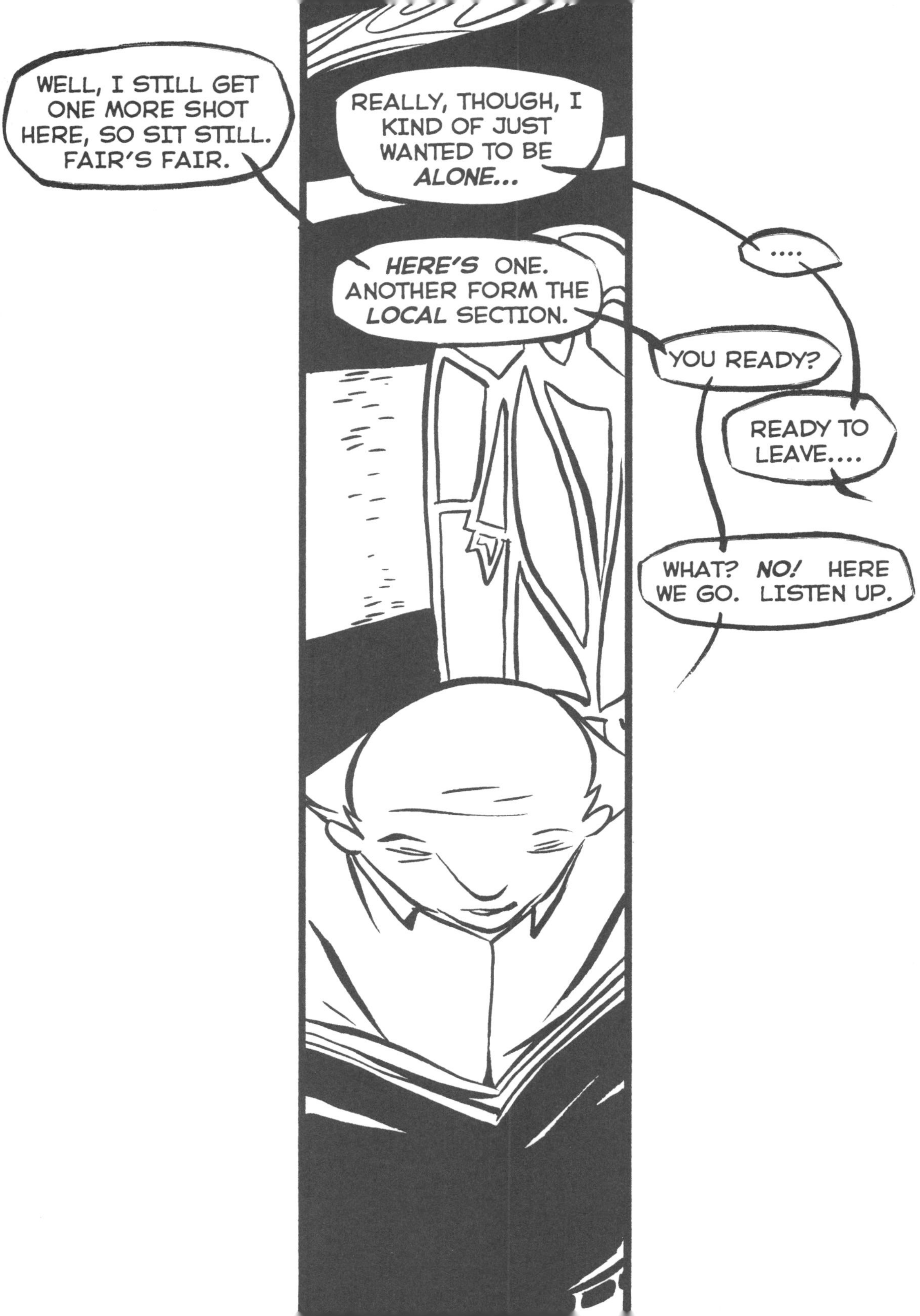
WELL, I STILL GET ONE MORE SHOT HERE, SO SIT STILL. FAIR'S FAIR.
REALLY, THOUGH, I KIND OF JUST WANTED TO BE ALONE...
....
HERE'S ONE. ANOTHER FORM THE LOCAL SECTION.
YOU READY?
READY TO LEAVE....
WHAT? NO! HERE WE GO. LISTEN UP.

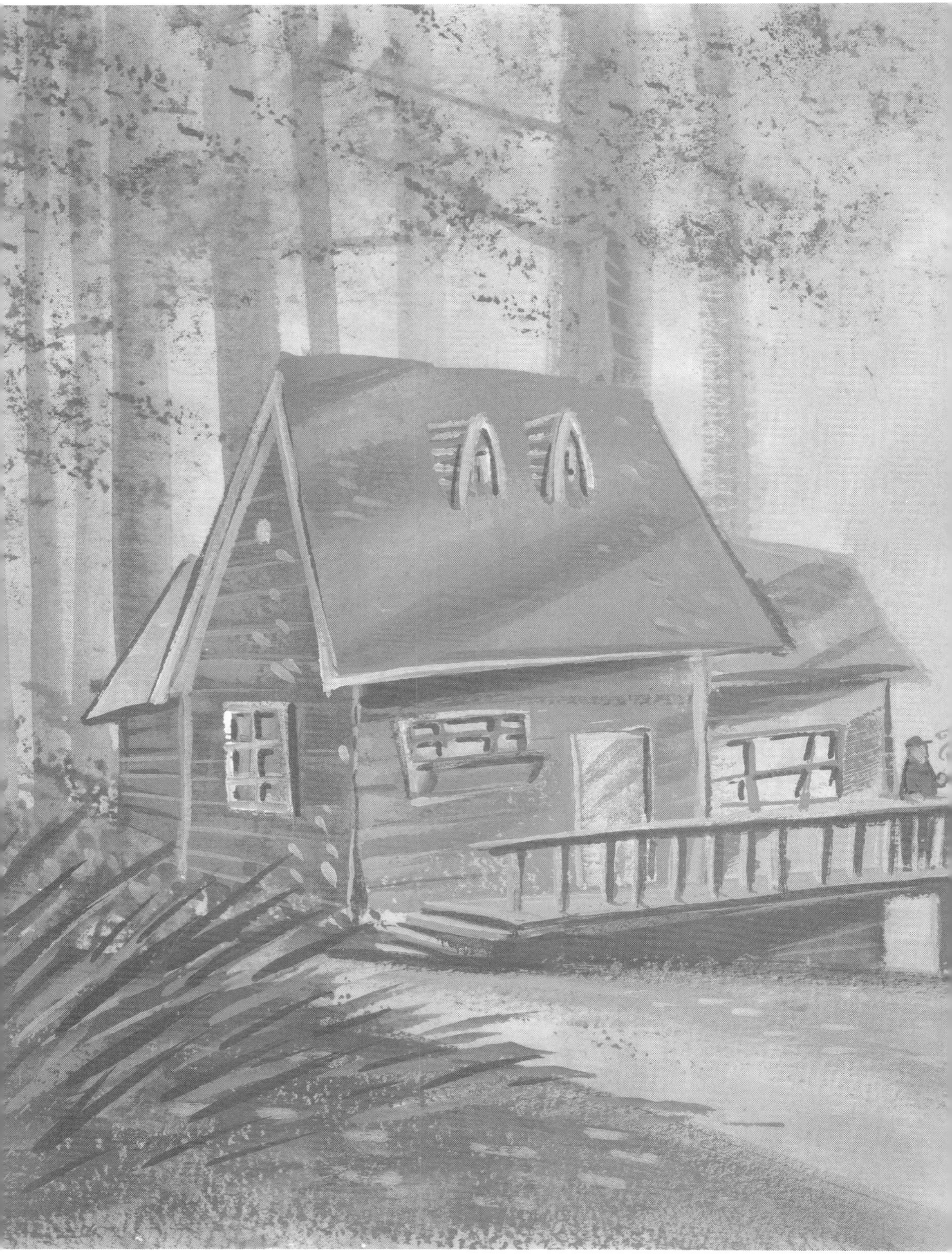

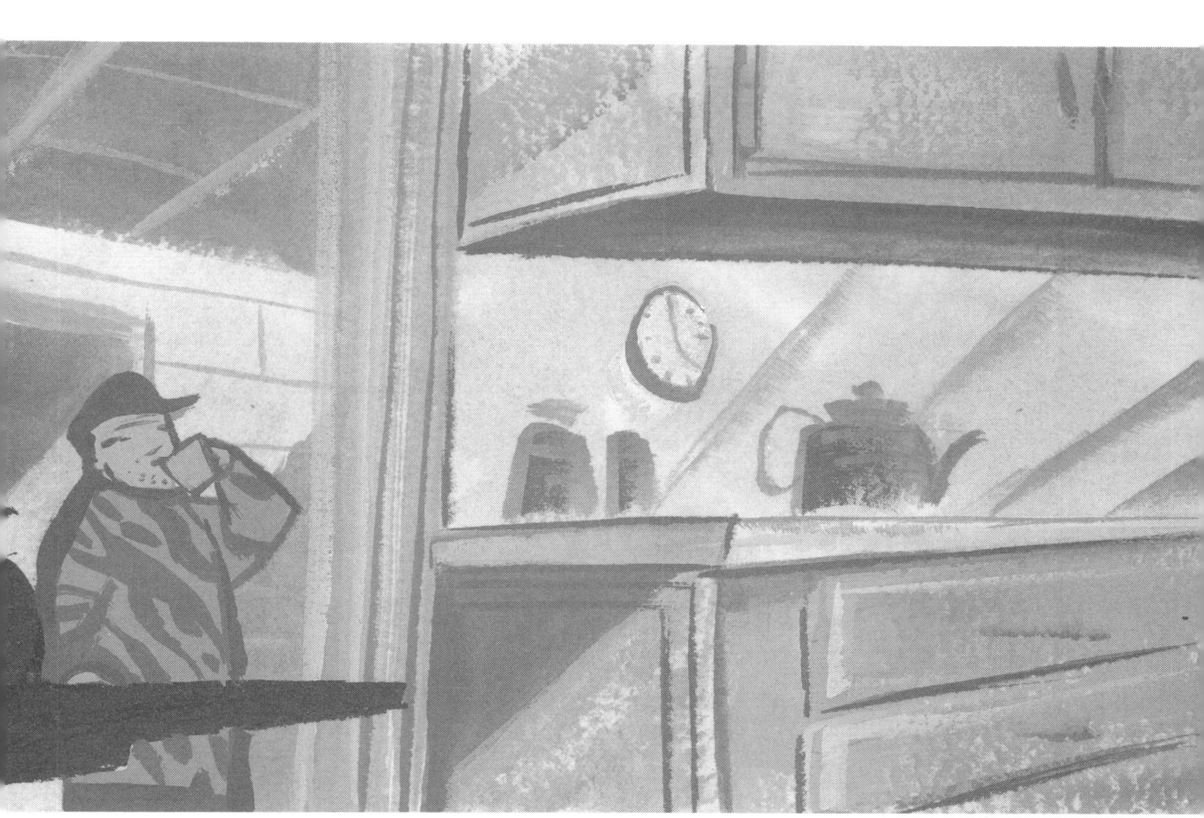

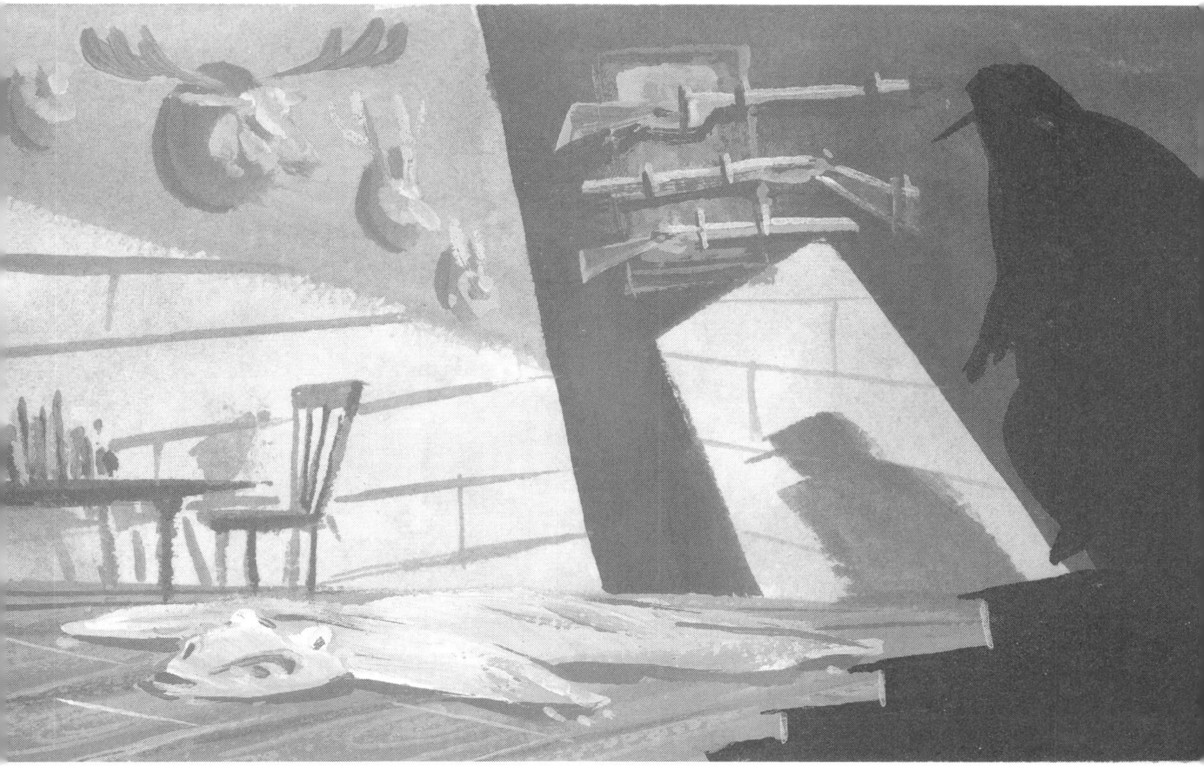

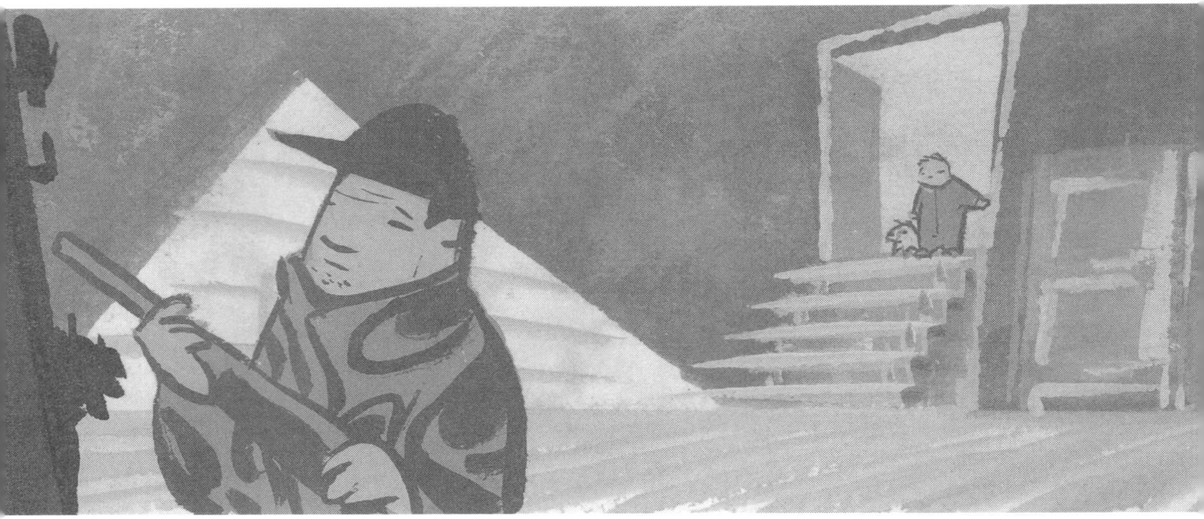

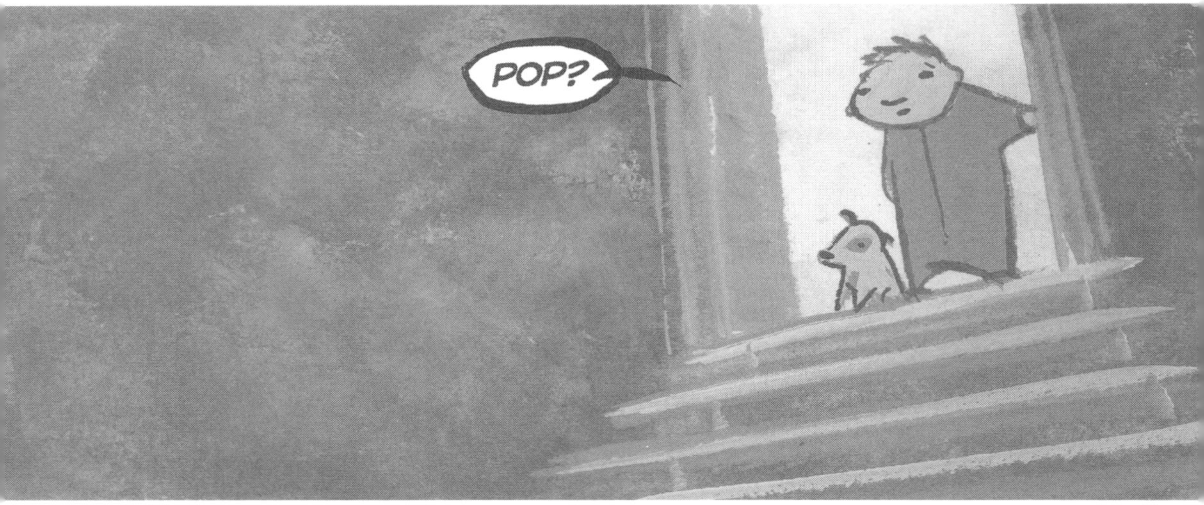
POP?

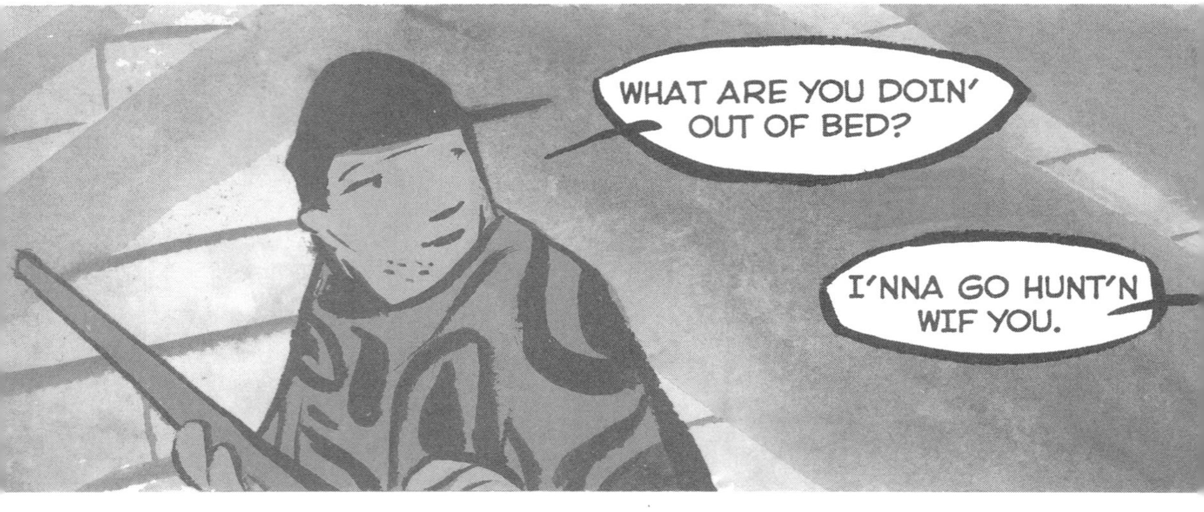
WHAT ARE YOU DOIN' OUT OF BED?
I'NNA GO HUNT'N WIF YOU.

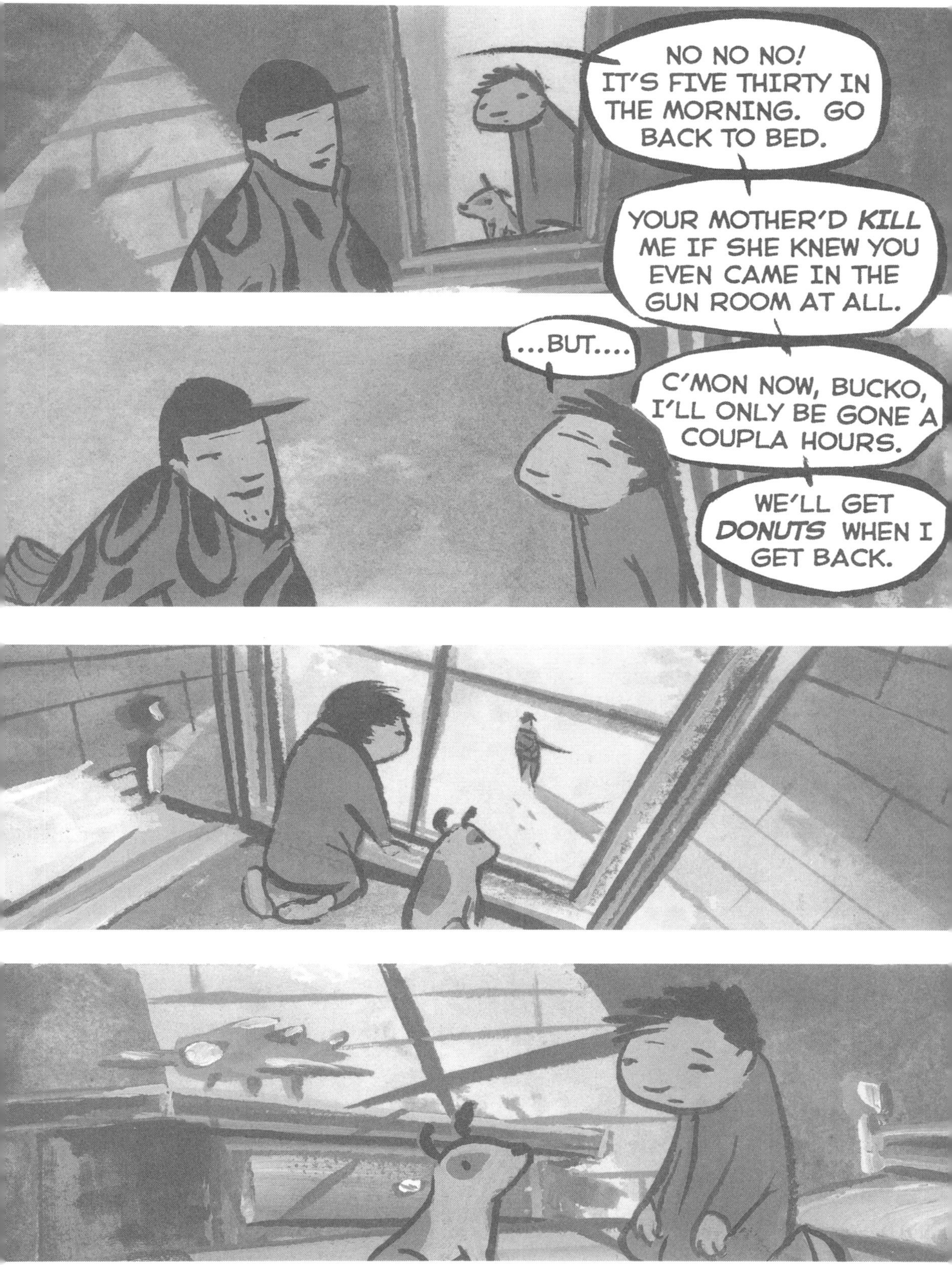
NO NO NO! IT'S FIVE THIRTY IN THE MORNING. GO BACK TO BED.
YOUR MOTHER'D KILL ME IF SHE KNEW YOU EVEN CAME IN THE GUN ROOM AT ALL.
...BUT....
C'MON NOW, BUCKO, I'LL ONLY BE GONE A COUPLA HOURS.
WE'LL GET DONUTS WHEN I GET BACK.

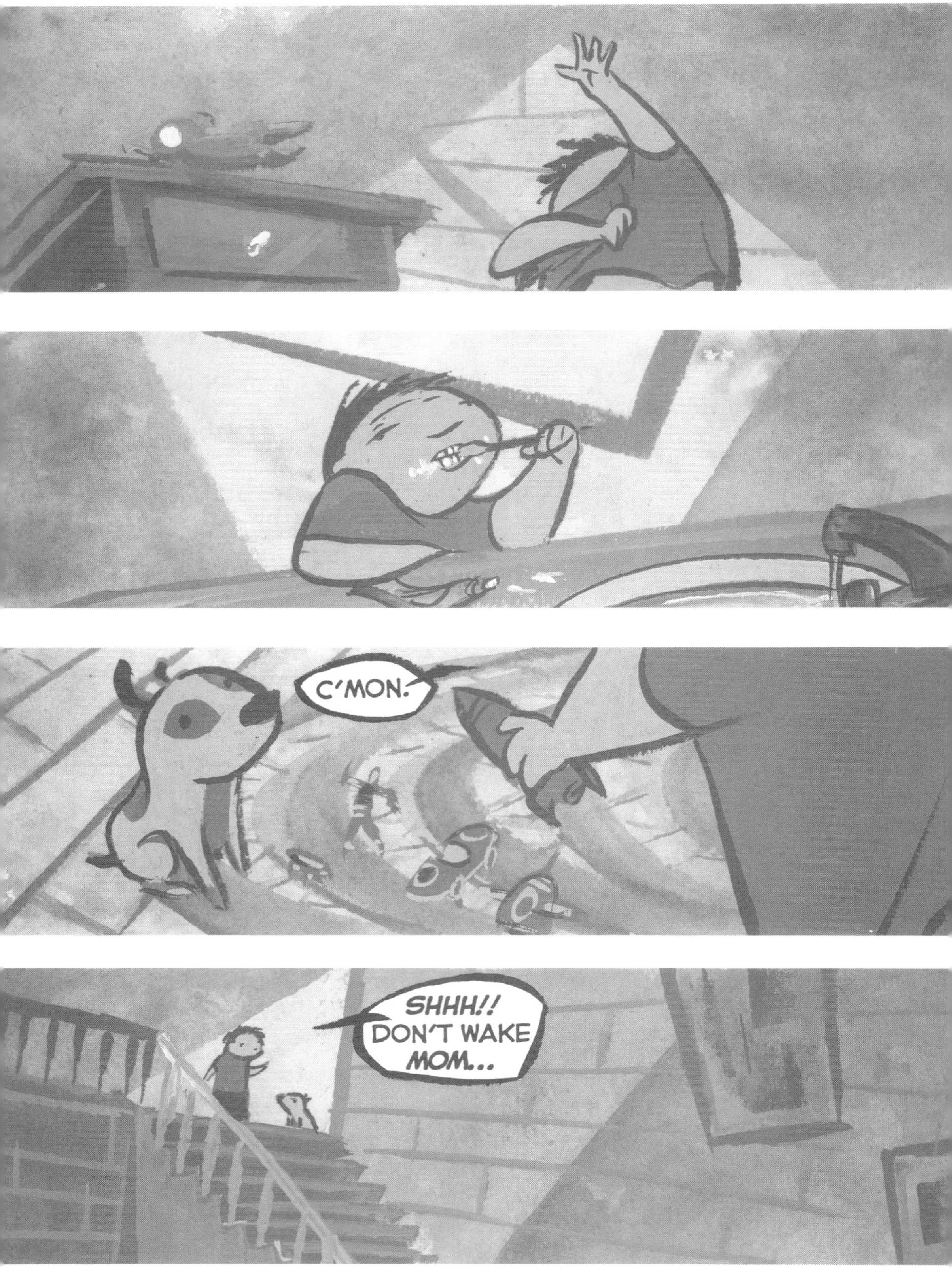
C'MON.
SHHH!! DON'T WAKE MOM...

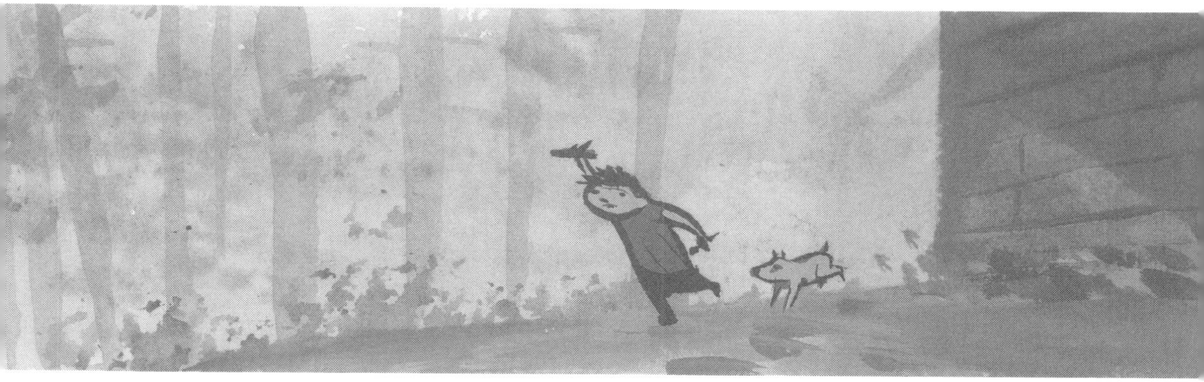

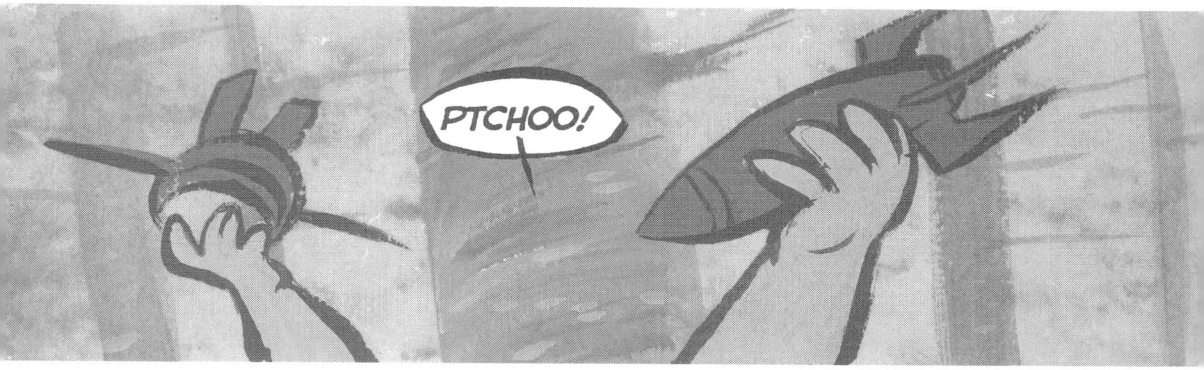
PTCHOO!

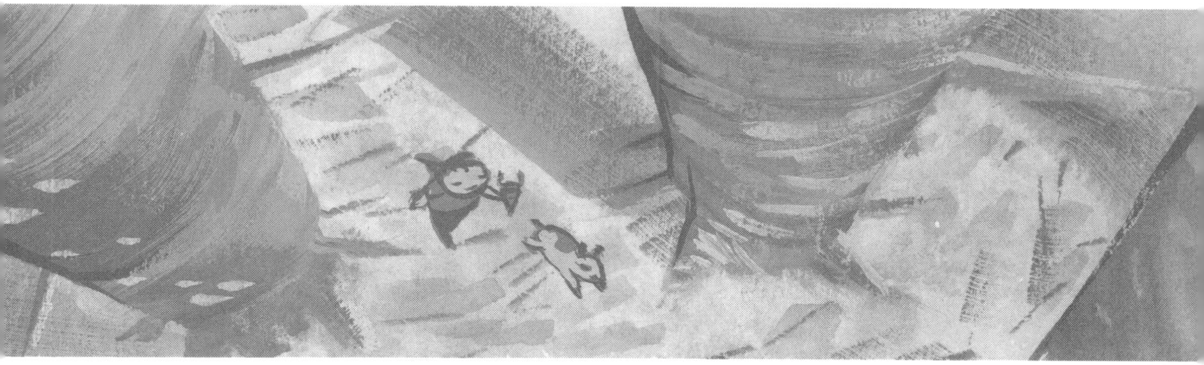

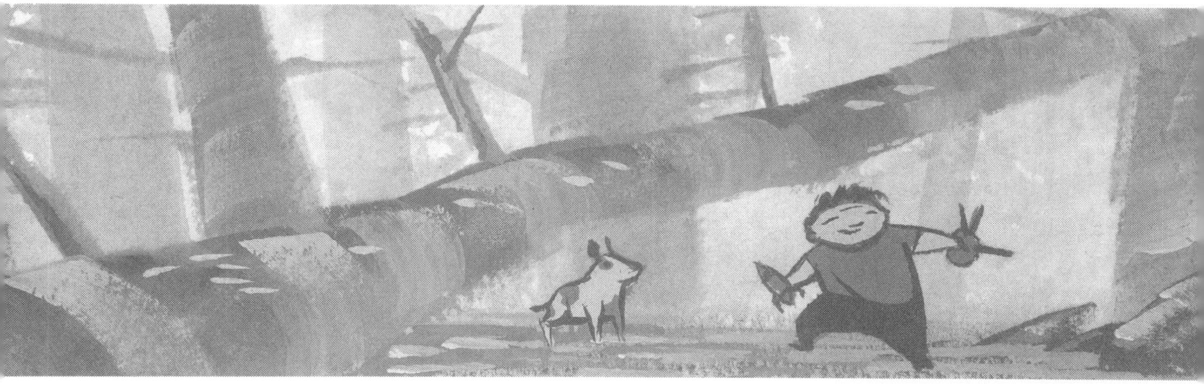

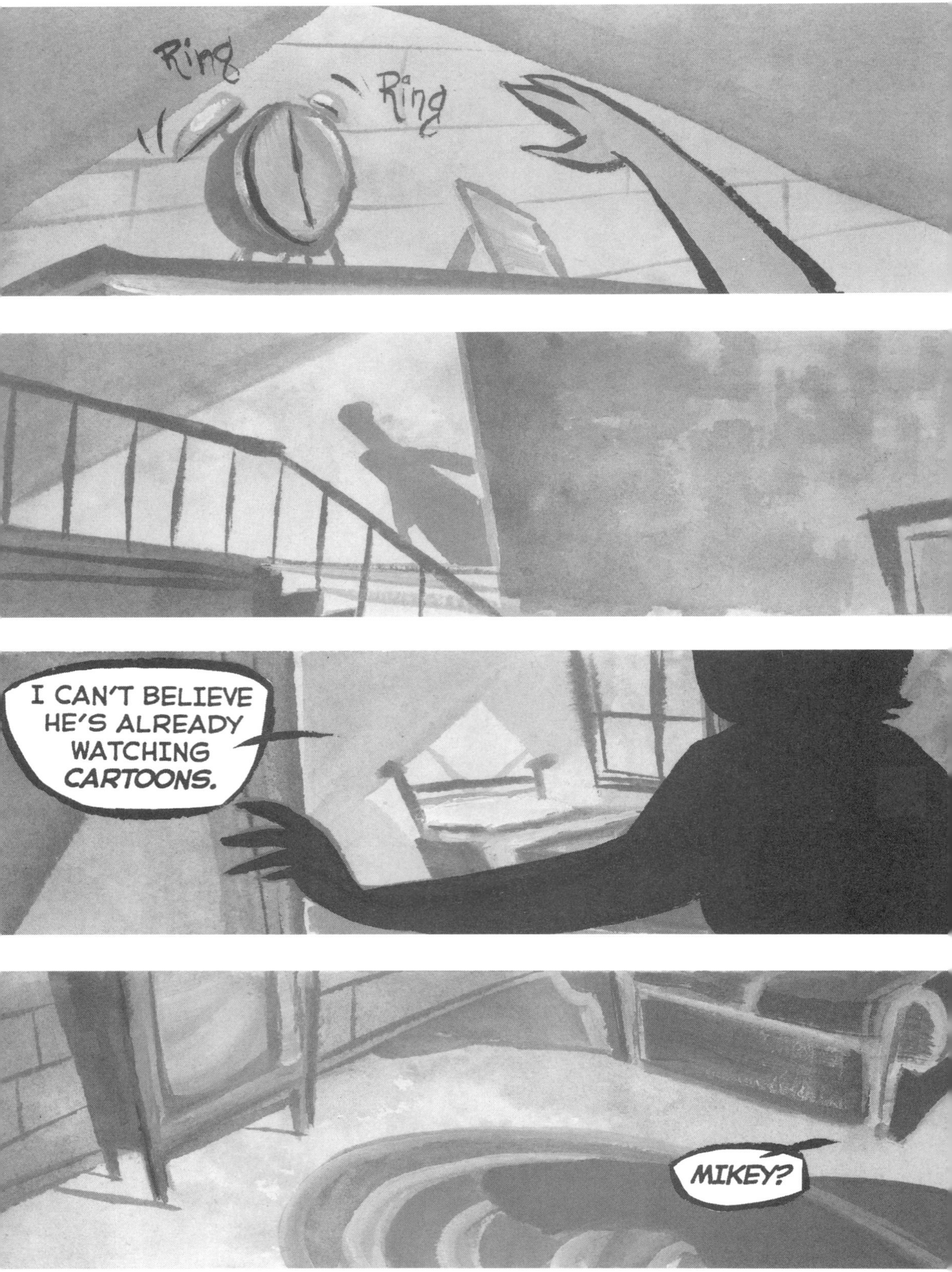
Ring
Ring
I CAN'T BELIEVE HE'S ALREADY WATCHING *CARTOONS.*
MIKEY?

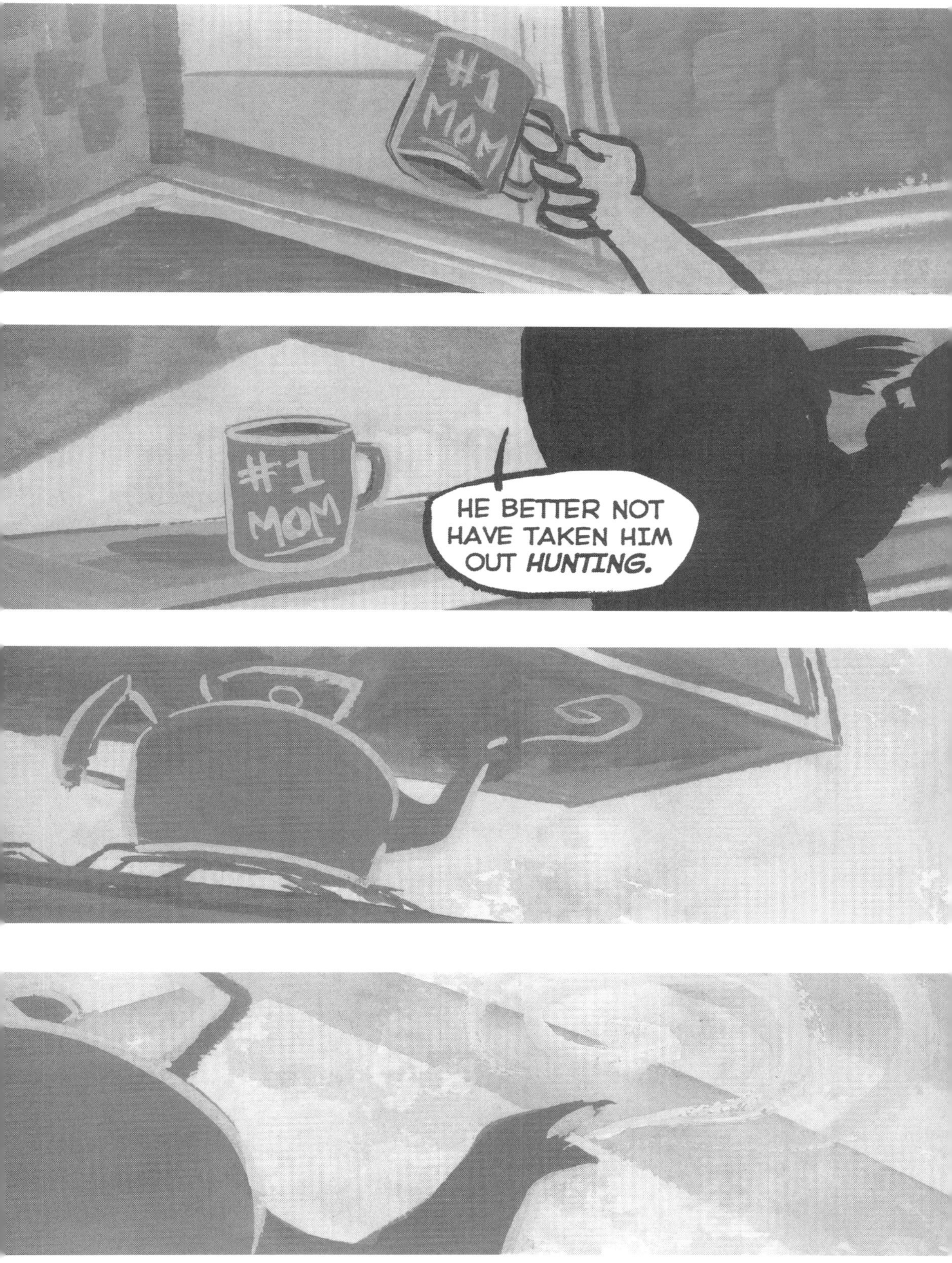
#1 MOM
#1 MOM
HE BETTER NOT HAVE TAKEN HIM OUT *HUNTING.*

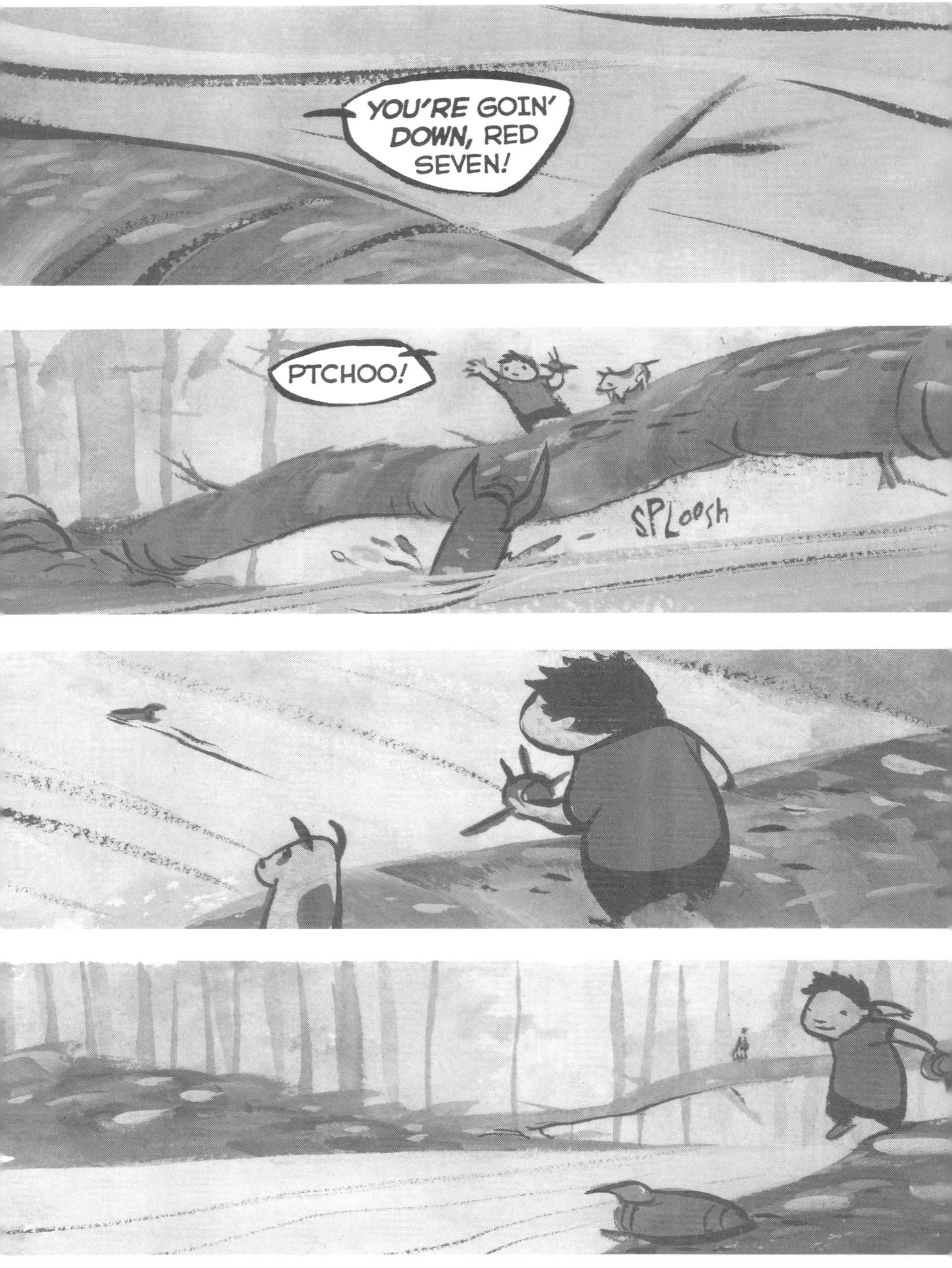
YOU'RE GOIN' DOWN, RED SEVEN!
PTCHOO!
SPLOOSH

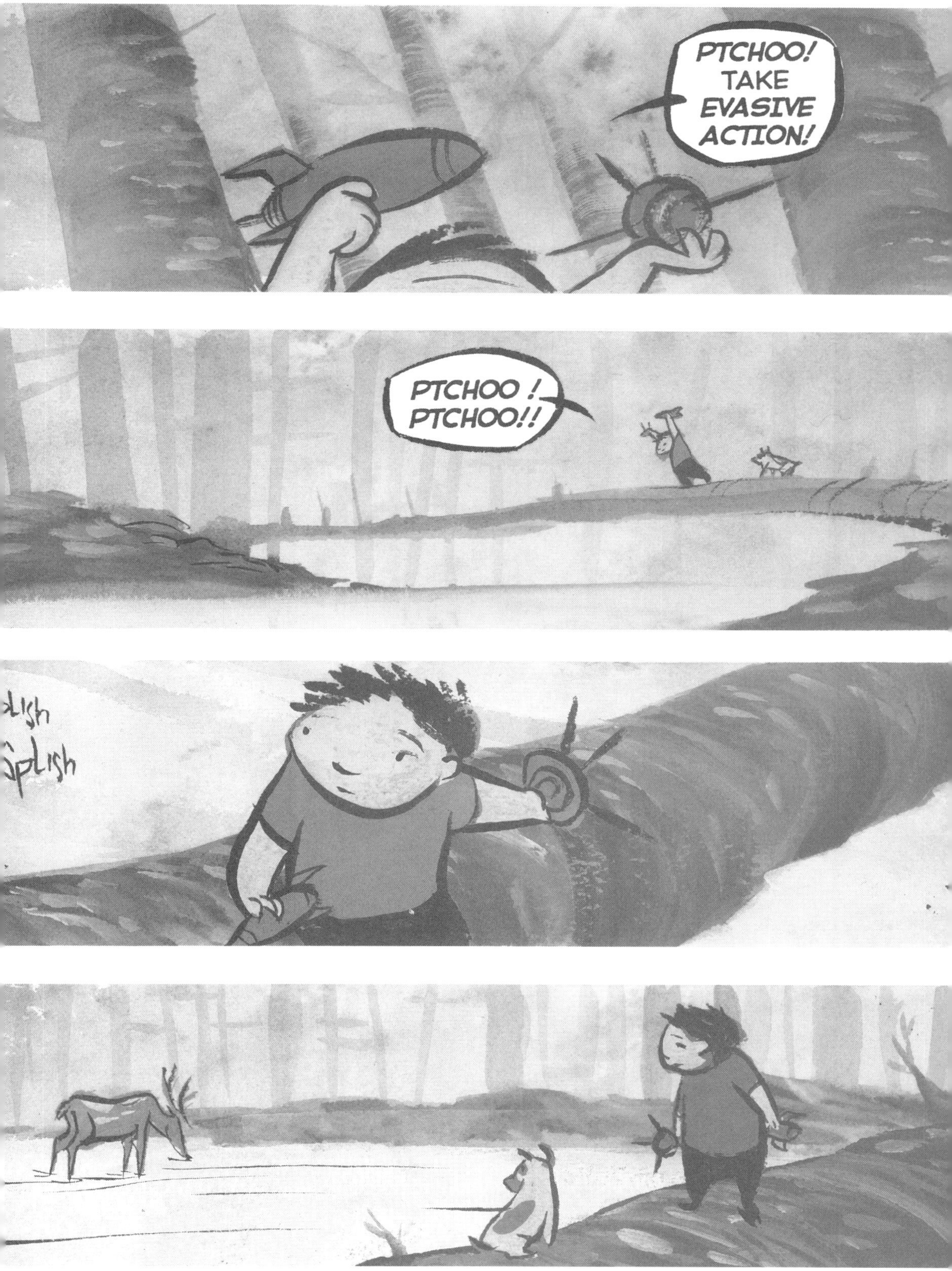
PTCHOO! TAKE EVASIVE ACTION!
PTCHOO ! PTCHOO!!
Splish

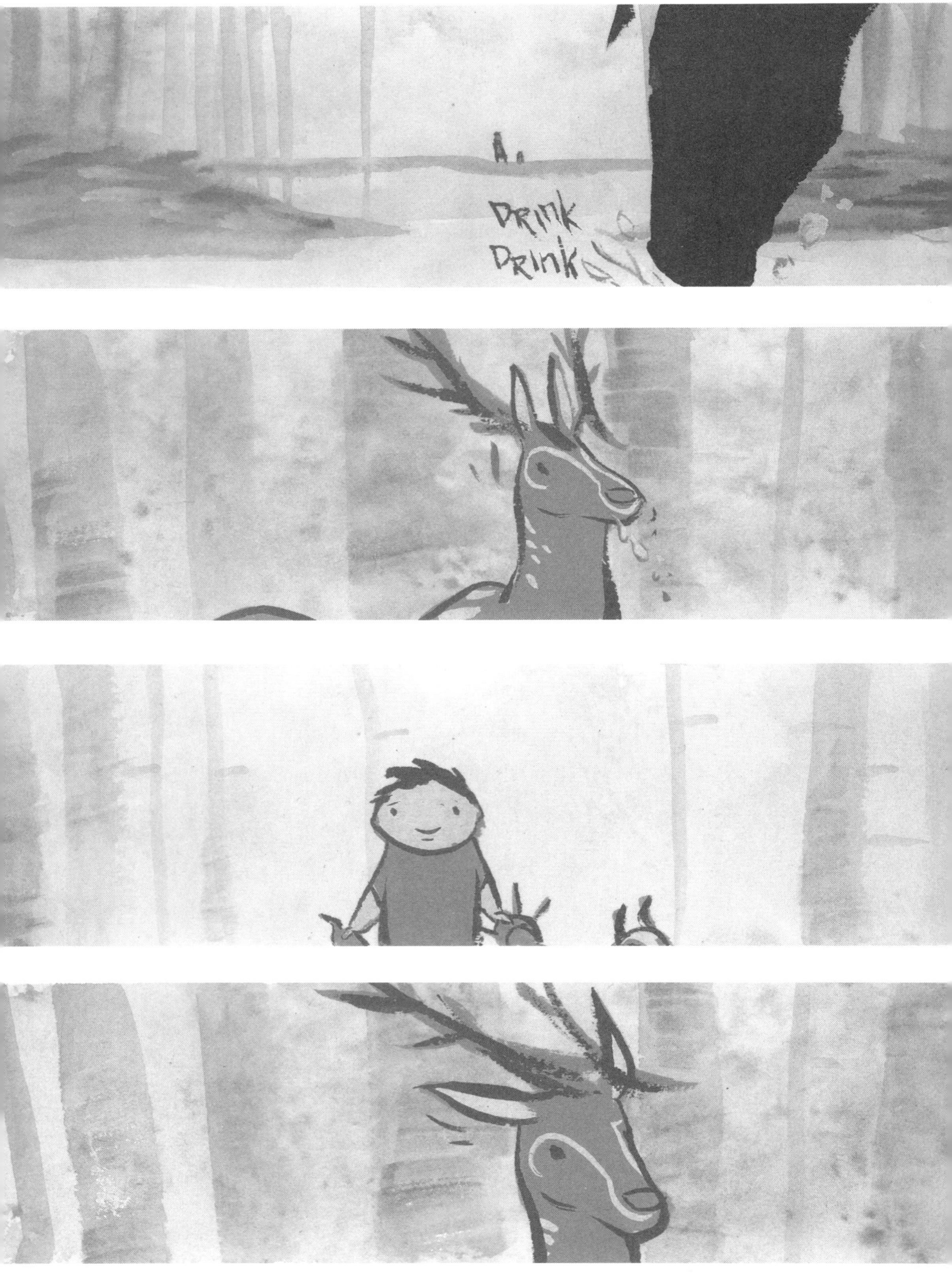
DRINK
DRINK

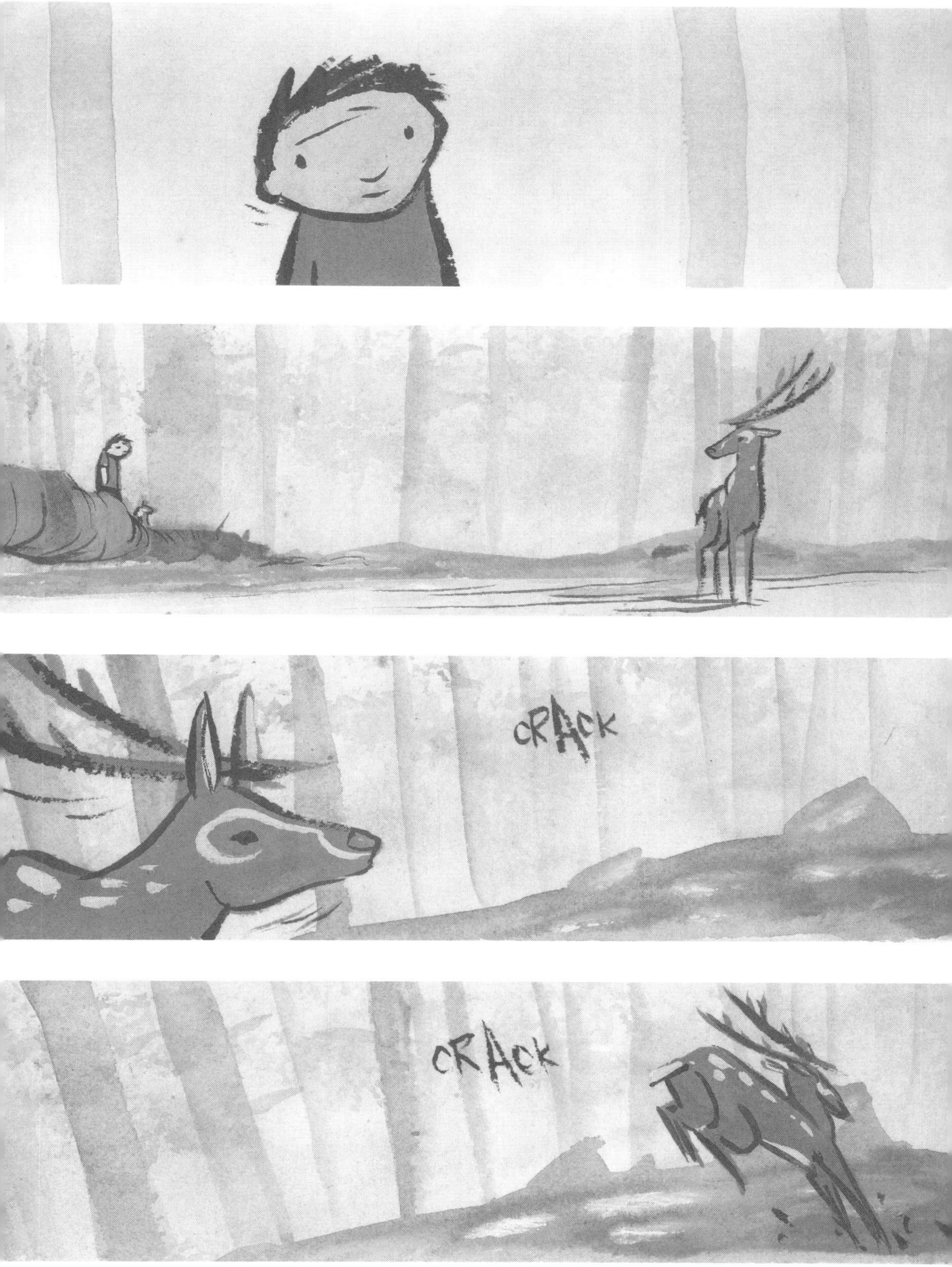
CRACK
CRACK

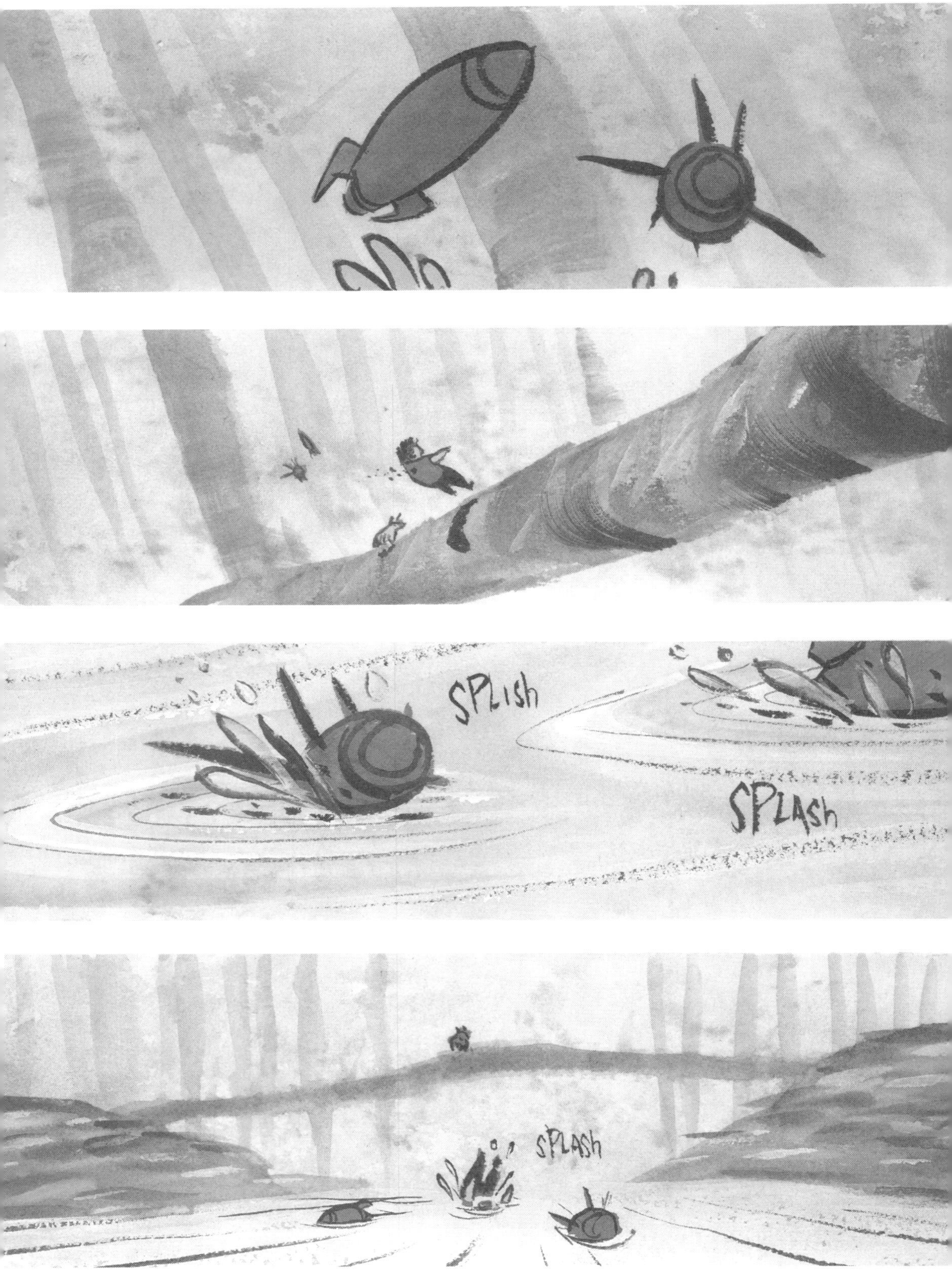
SPLish
SPLASh
SPLASh

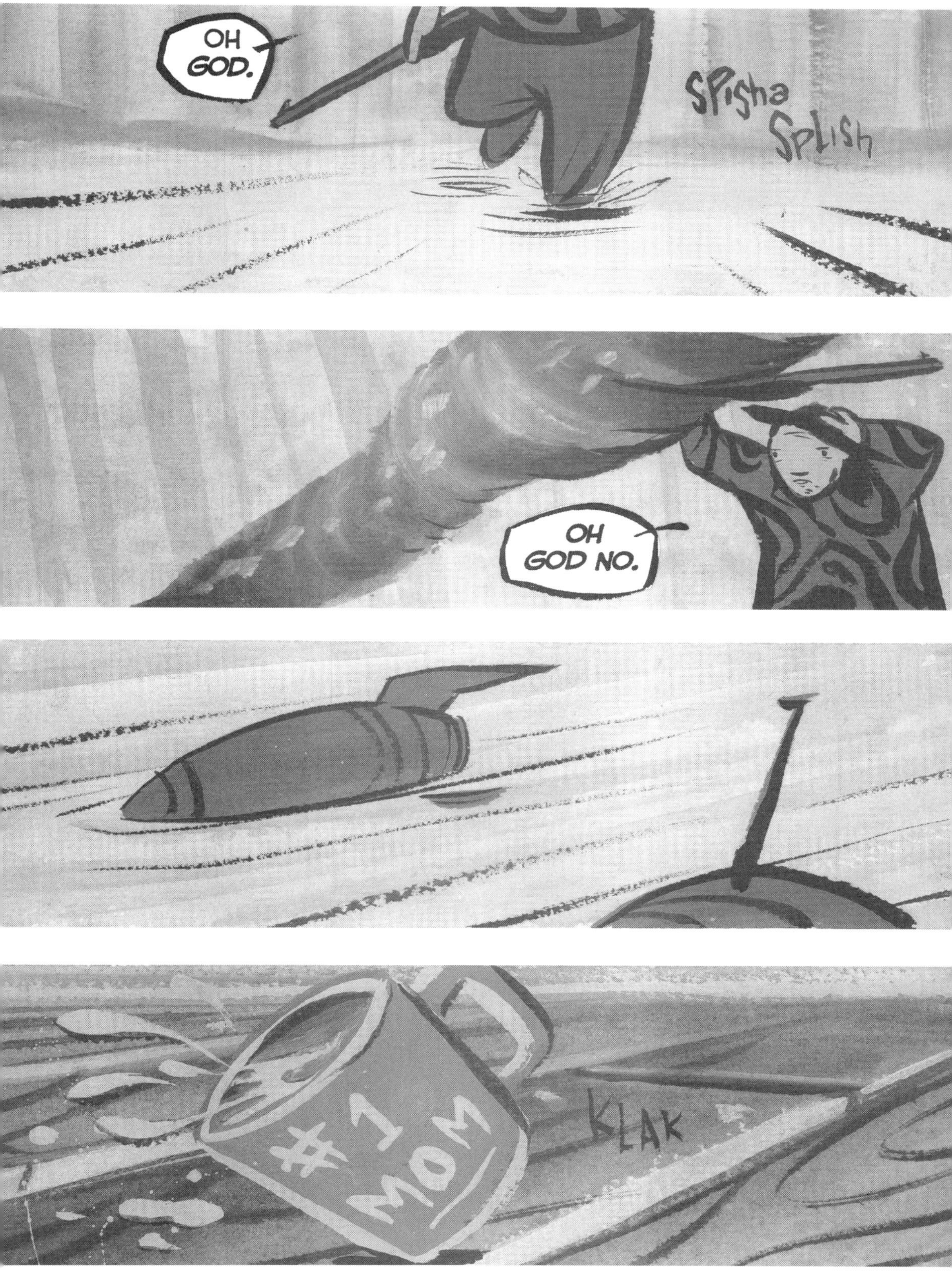
OH GOD.
SPISHA
SPLISH
OH GOD NO.
#1 MOM
KLAK

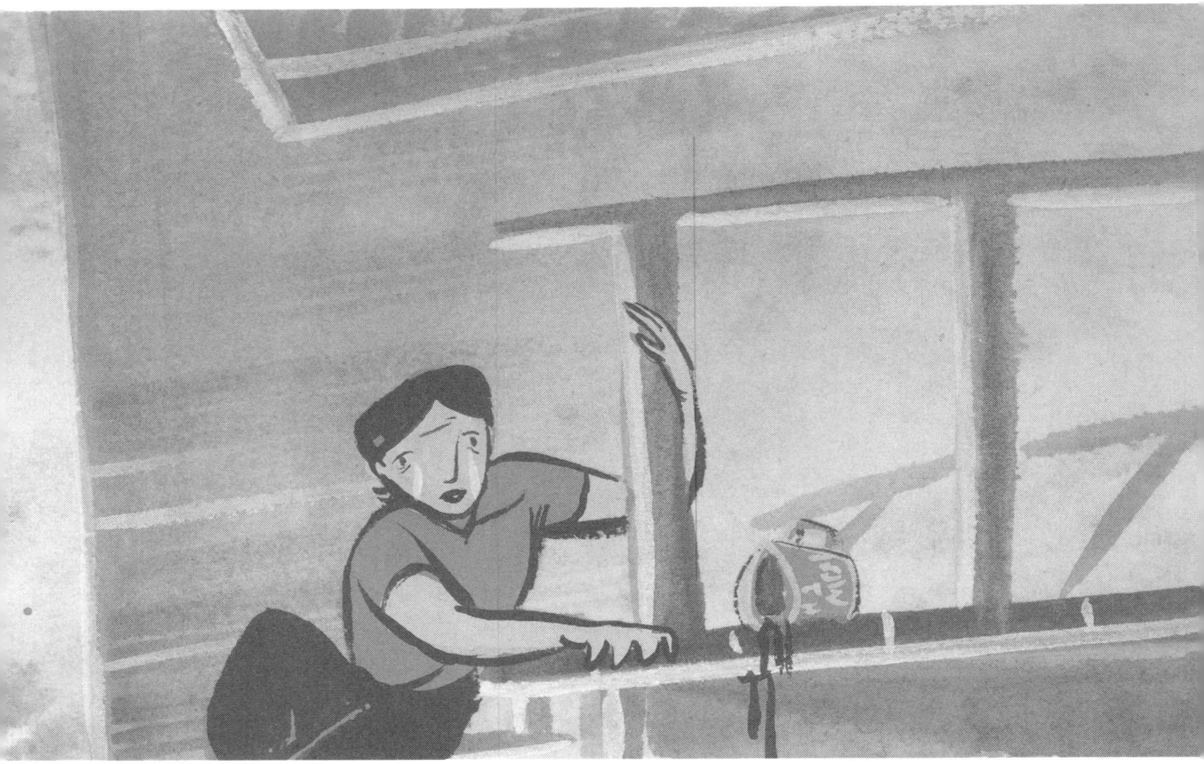

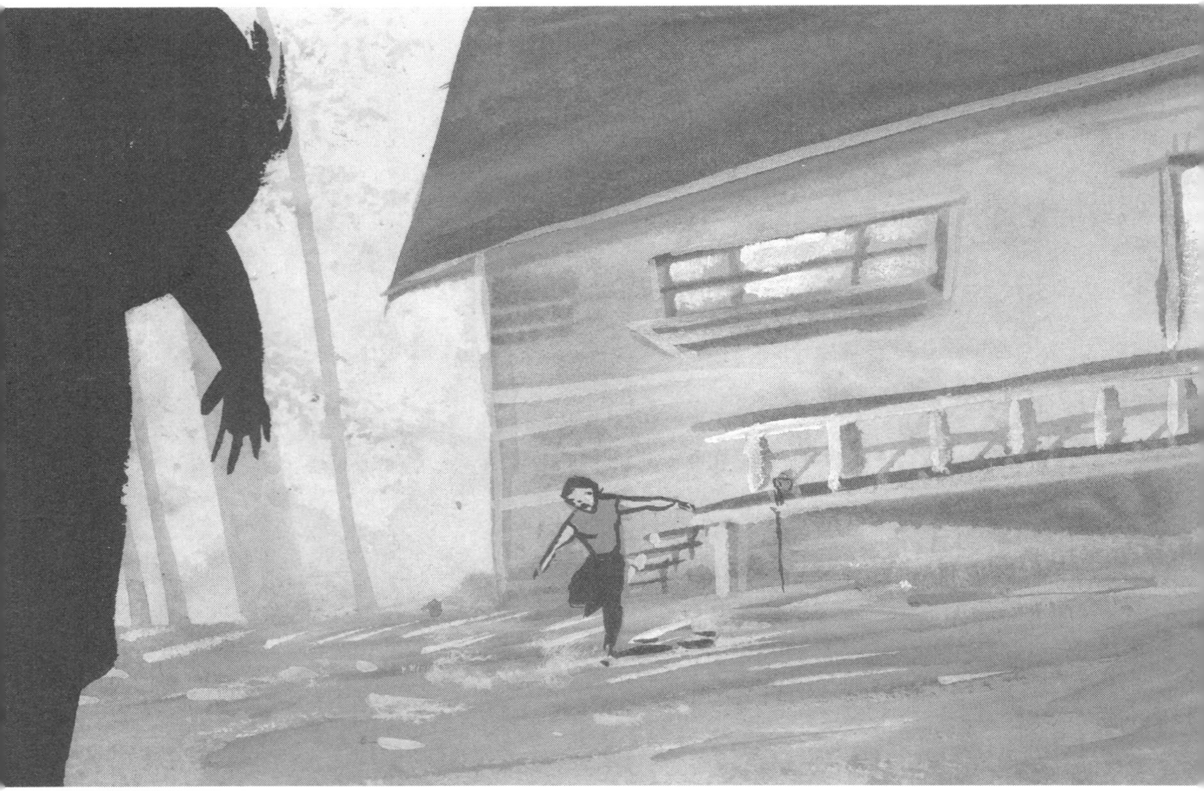

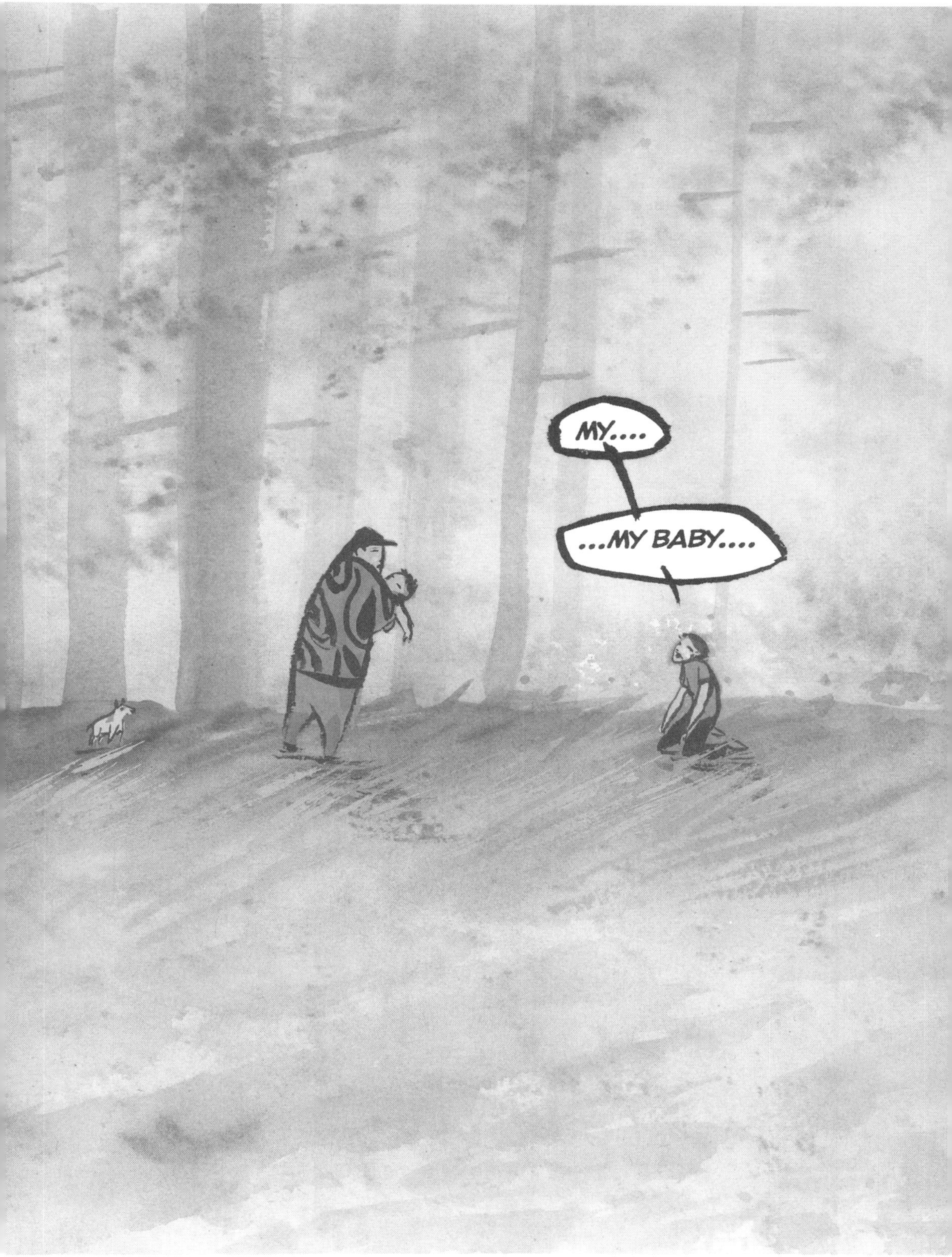
MY....
...MY BABY....

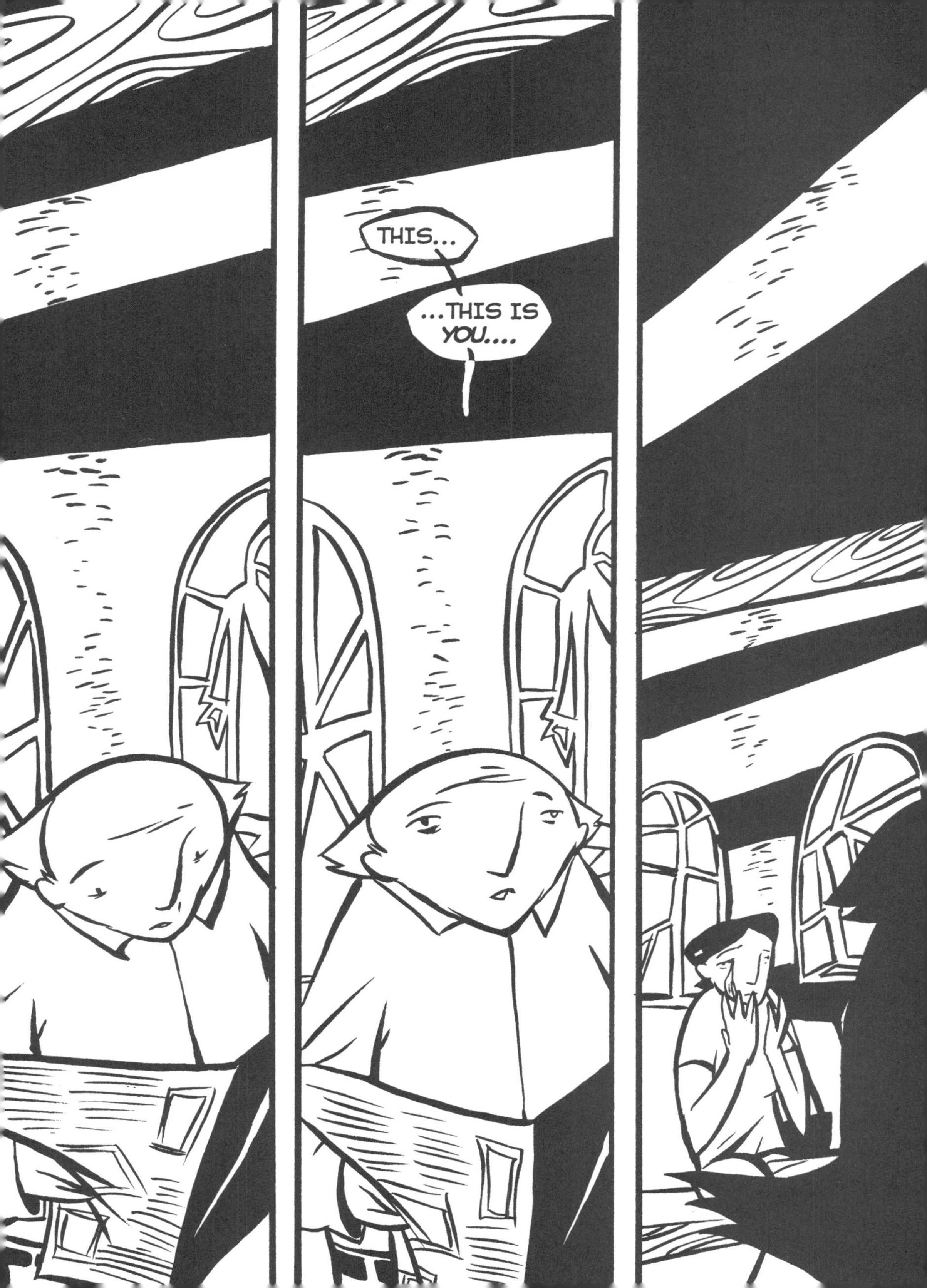
THIS...
...THIS IS YOU....

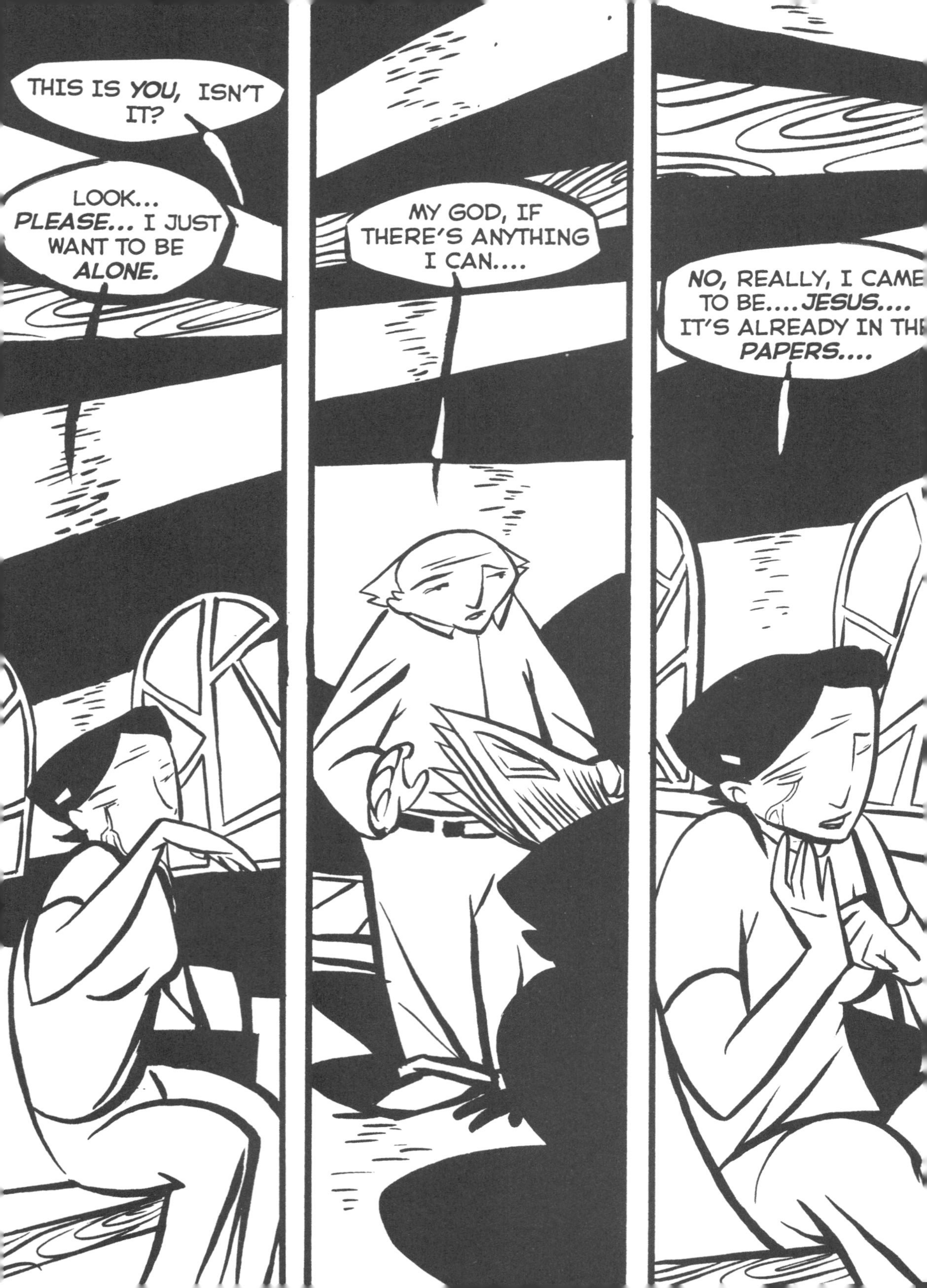
THIS IS *YOU,* ISN'T IT?
LOOK... *PLEASE...* I JUST WANT TO BE *ALONE.*
MY GOD, IF THERE'S ANYTHING I CAN....
NO, REALLY, I CAME TO BE.... *JESUS....* IT'S ALREADY IN THE *PAPERS....*

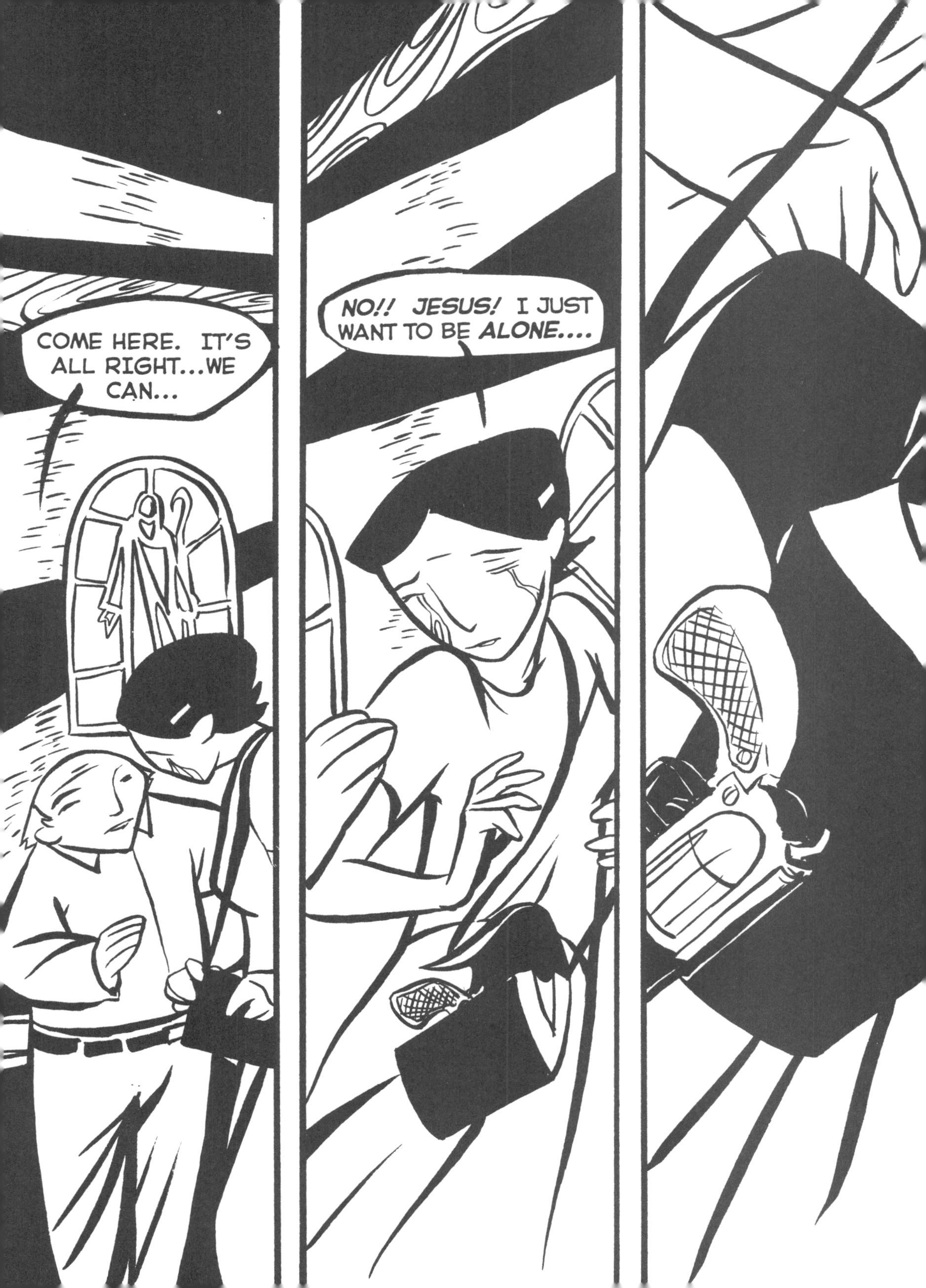
COME HERE. IT'S ALL RIGHT...WE CAN...
NO!! JESUS! I JUST WANT TO BE ALONE....

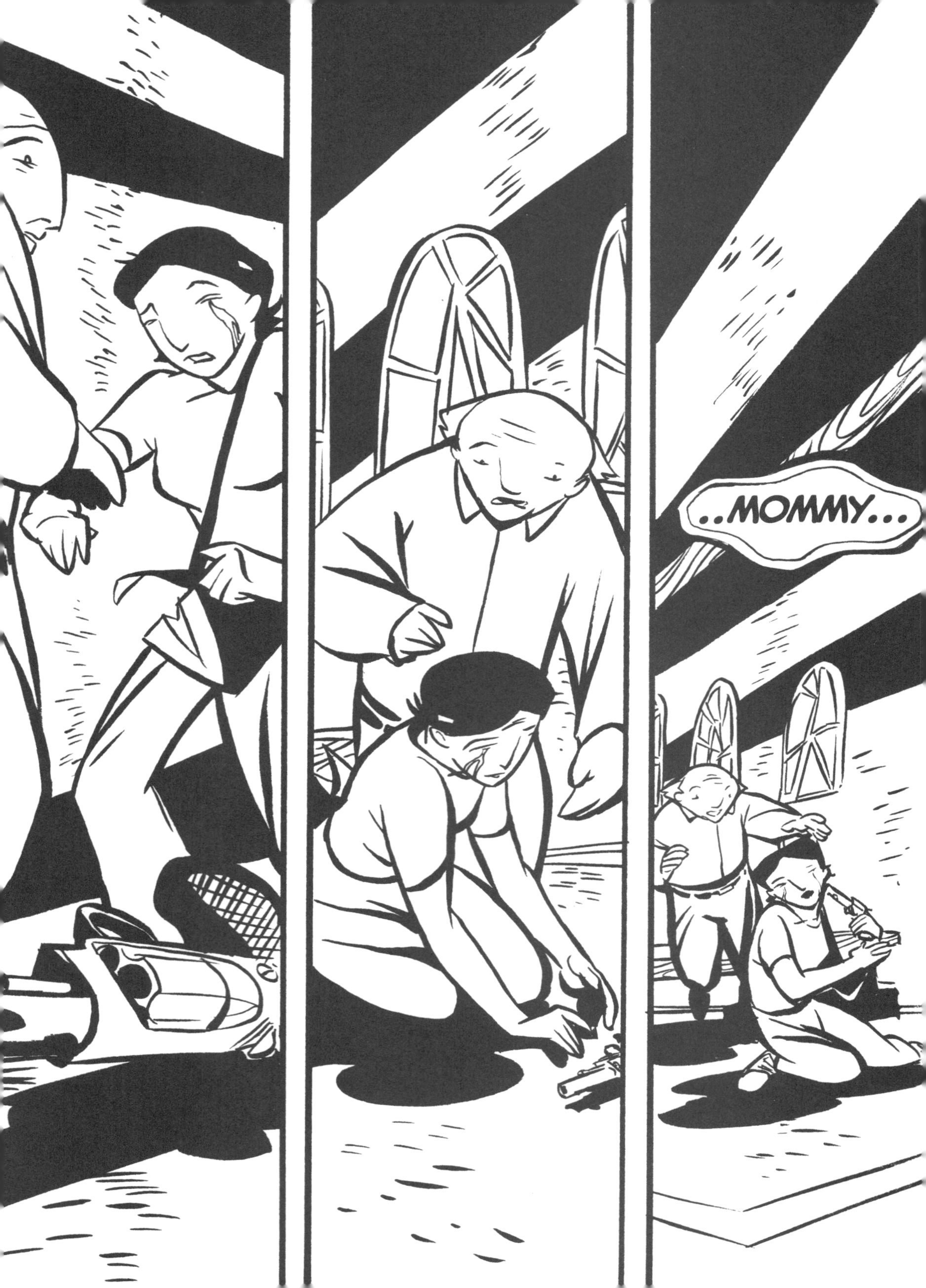
..MOMMY...

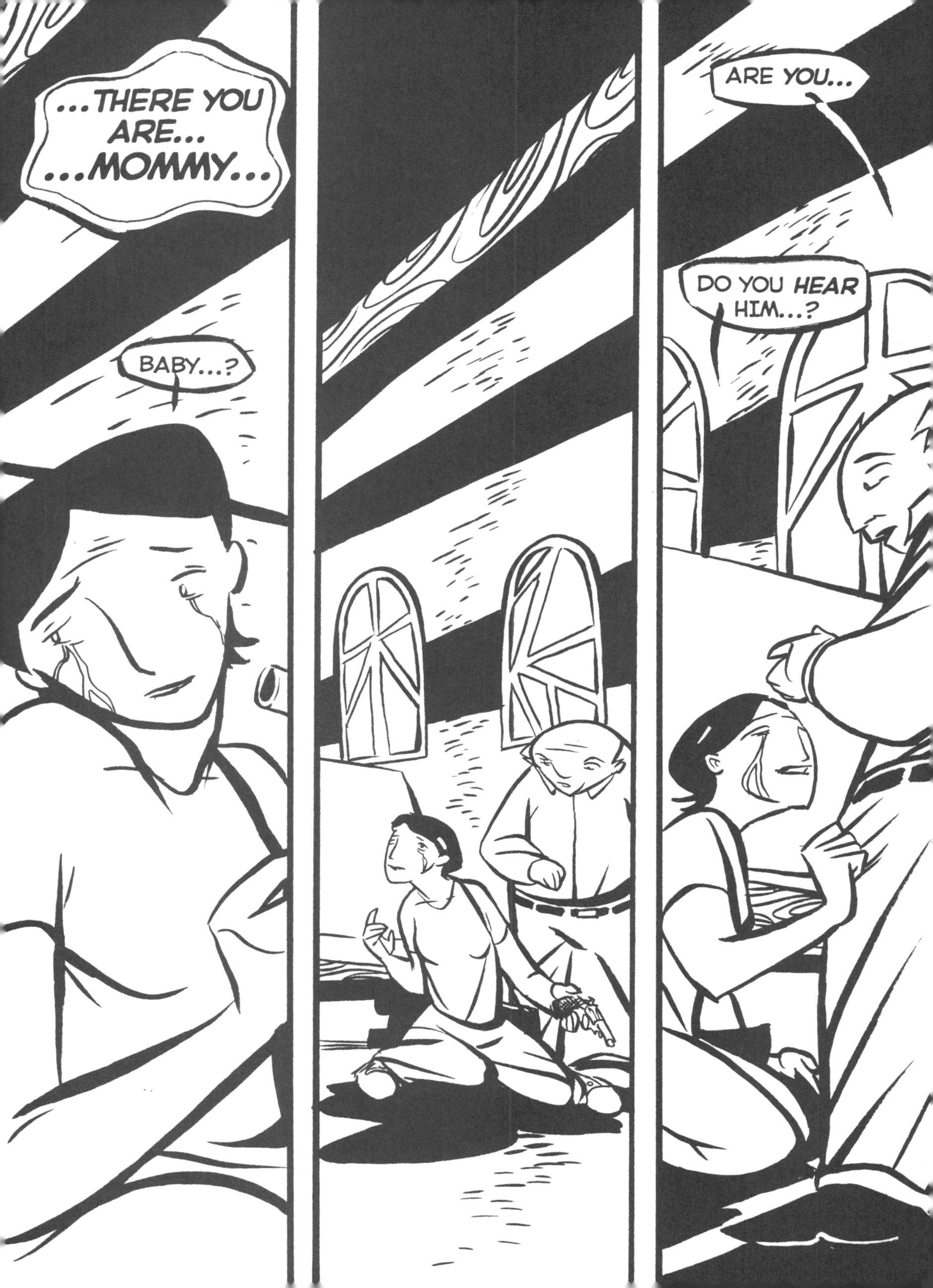
...THERE YOU ARE... ...MOMMY...
BABY...?
ARE YOU...
DO YOU HEAR HIM...?

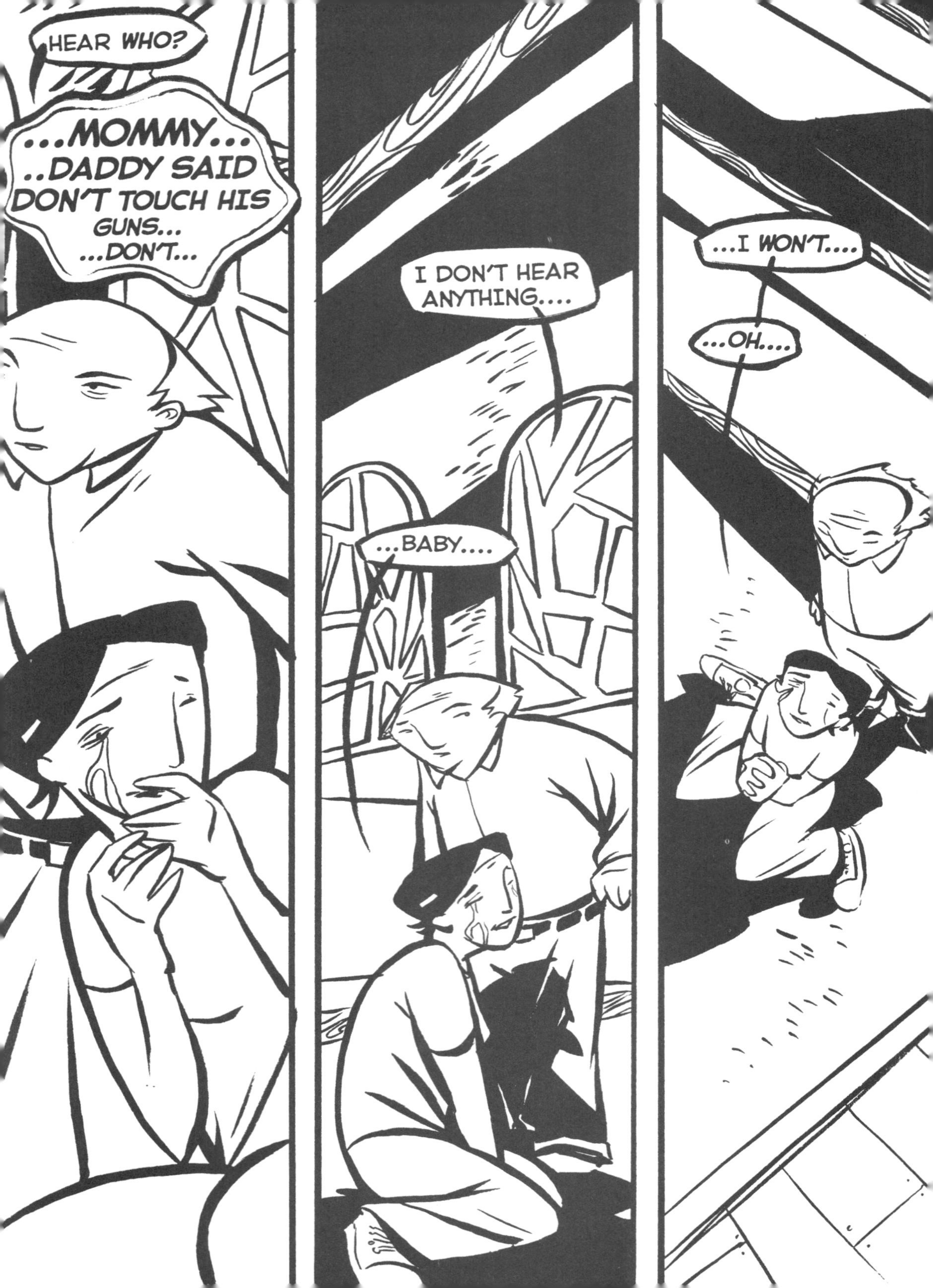
HEAR WHO?
...MOMMY...
..DADDY SAID DON'T TOUCH HIS GUNS...
...DON'T...
I DON'T HEAR ANYTHING....
...BABY....
...I WON'T....
...OH....

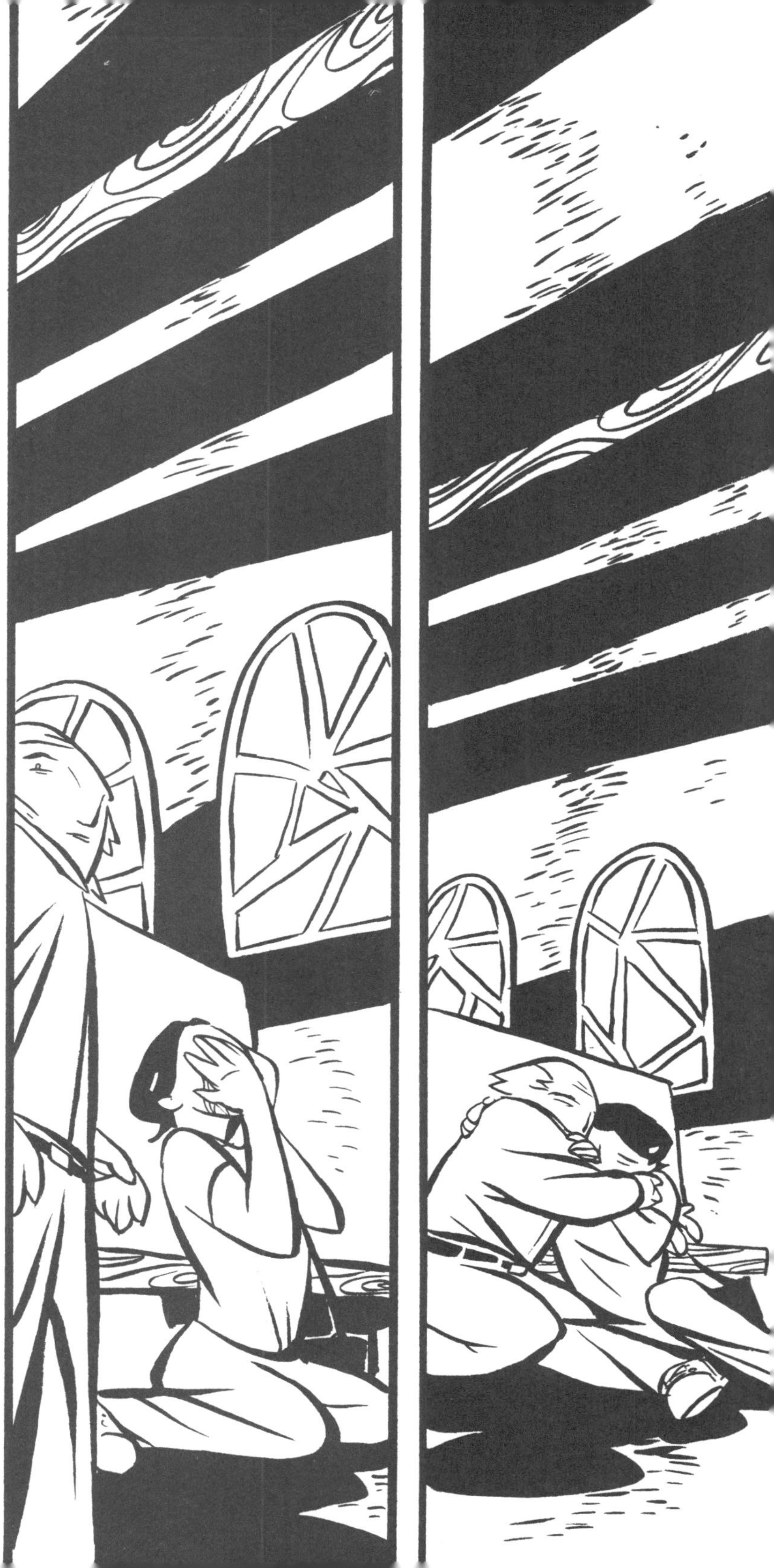

Other books from Oni Press and Scott Morse...

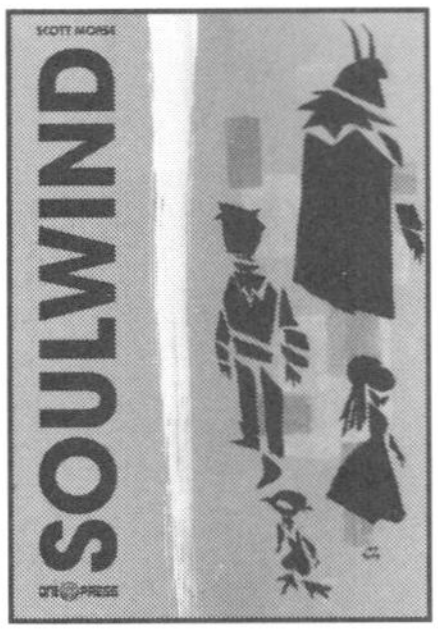
SOULWIND

THE COMPLETE SOULWIND™
520 pages,
black-and-white interiors
$29.95 US, $46.95 CAN
ISBN: 1-92999873-2
Available November, 2003.

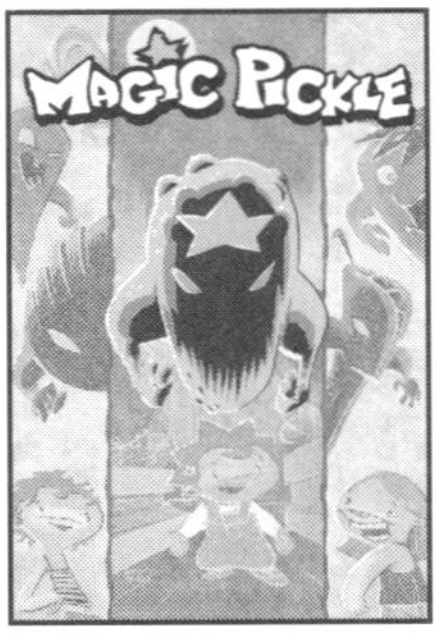
MAGIC PICKLE

MAGIC PICKLE™
128 pages,
black-and-white interiors
$11.95 us, $17.95 CAN
ISBN: 1-929998-33-3

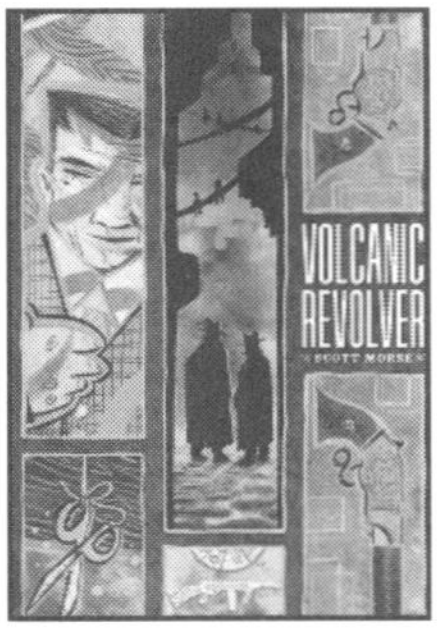
VOLCANIC REVOLVER
SCOTT MORSE

VOLCANIC REVOLVER™
120 pages,
sepia-and-white interiors
$9.95 US, $15.95 CAN
ISBN: 1-09667127-5-7

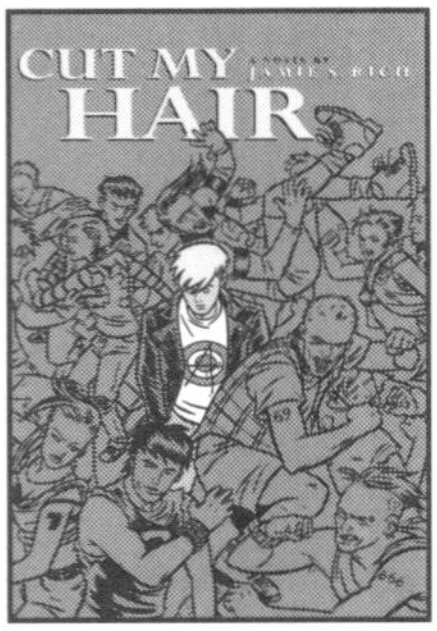
CUT MY HAIR

CUT MY HAIR™
by Jamie S. Rich
w/ Chynna Clugston-Major,
Scott Morse, Judd Winick,
& Andi Watson
236 pages, black-and-white
text with illustrations
$15.95 US, $23.95 CAN
ISBN: 0-9700387-0-4

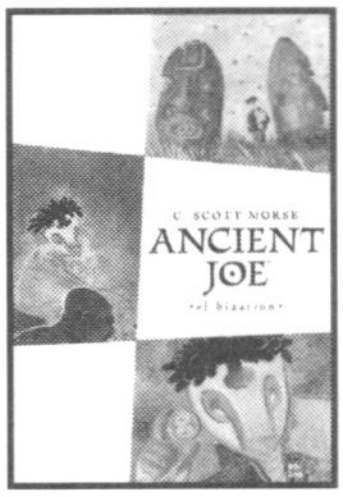
C. SCOTT MORSE
ANCIENT JOE

ANCIENT JOE™
120 pages, black-and-white
interiors
$12.95 US, $17.95 CAN
ISBN: 1-56971-795-8

Published by
Dark Horse Comics

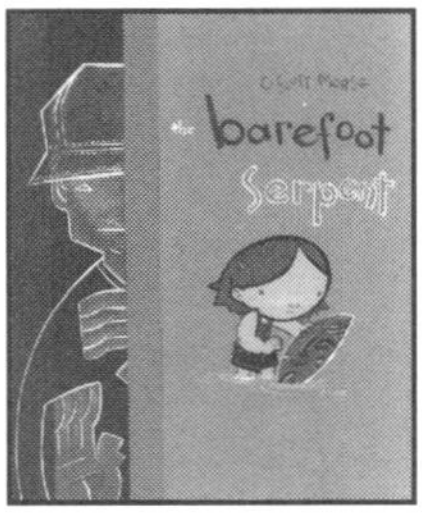
barefoot Serpent

BAREFOOT SERPENT™
96 pages black-and-white,
32 pages painted color
$14.95 US, $22.95 CAN
ISBN: 1-891830-37-6

Published by
Top Shelf Productions

Oni Press graphic novels are available at finer comics shops everywhere. For a comics store near you, call 1-888-COMIC-BOOK, or visit www.the-master-list.com.